KARL
LAGERFELD

For Sam Guelimi

KARL LAGERFELD

Véronique Bergen

Abrams, New York

SILHOUETTE   E/P/A

CONTENTS

Following spread:
Karl Lagerfeld, 2003.

HISTORY

History

Designer and stylist
Lagerfeld at his residence
in Monaco, August 1986.

Karl Lagerfeld was a fashion giant and a chameleon, a man firmly entrenched behind masks of his own creation. He made the Cartesian motto *Larvatus prodeo* ("I go forth masked") one of his life's principles. A stylist, photographer, designer, and publisher, the so-called "kaiser of fashion" never ceased to fictionalize the story of his life. He continually sowed doubt about his date of birth and recast his German origins, wishing to both remain an enigma and build his legend. The art with which Lagerfeld rewrote his life—hiding himself almost literally behind a suit of armor—formed a kind of aesthetic of alteration.

Still, looking past the eccentric and romantic details with which he adorned his youth, the concealment of his family situation, and the character that he created—where he was both the puppeteer and the puppet—a few facts can be ascertained. Karl Otto Lagerfeld was born on September 10, 1933, in Hamburg, Germany, and died on February 19, 2019, in Neuilly-sur-Seine, just outside of Paris. The son of Otto Lagerfeld, an industrialist who made his fortune in the dairy sector, and Elisabeth Bahlmann, who had a decisive influence on his life, Lagerfeld developed a passion for drawing from childhood. He first lived with his family in an upscale district of Hamburg—together with his sister, Martha-Christiane, and his half-sister, Théa—until the Allied bombings

of 1943, known as Operation Gomorrah, which destroyed much of the city. From then on, the Lagerfelds took refuge in the north, on their family estate near Bad Bramstedt.

A solitary child, young Karl was fond of books and prone to daydreaming. He was already drawn toward elegance, and he largely kept to himself. He learned to read at the age of five, and by ten was reading Balzac's *Béatrix* in French and studying foreign languages. His true vocation came to light in 1949, when the Lagerfelds returned to Hamburg after the end of World War II. After the shame of Nazi Germany and the horror and tragedy of the Holocaust, the fashion world intended to help turn the page and blow in a fresh wind of freedom. The days of rationing and fabric shortages were over, and haute couture was back in the spotlight.

On December 13, at the age of sixteen, Lagerfeld went with his mother to the Esplanade Hotel to see his first fashion show. The designer was Christian Dior, and it was both an aesthetic shock and an epiphany for Lagerfeld. Just a few years before, in 1947, Dior had breathed fresh life into fashion with what the editor in chief of *Harper's Bazaar* had called the "New Look." Gone were the austere, utilitarian outfits of wartime. Dior revolutionized both femininity and the female silhouette, offering narrow, fitted jackets with rounded

Above:
Lagerfeld circa 1960.

Right:
At the VIP Room nightclub in Saint-Tropez, August 2009.

Following spread:
Lagerfeld and Gisele Bündchen, Chanel spring/summer 2015 ready-to-wear collection, Paris Fashion Week, September 2014.

KARL LAGERFELD

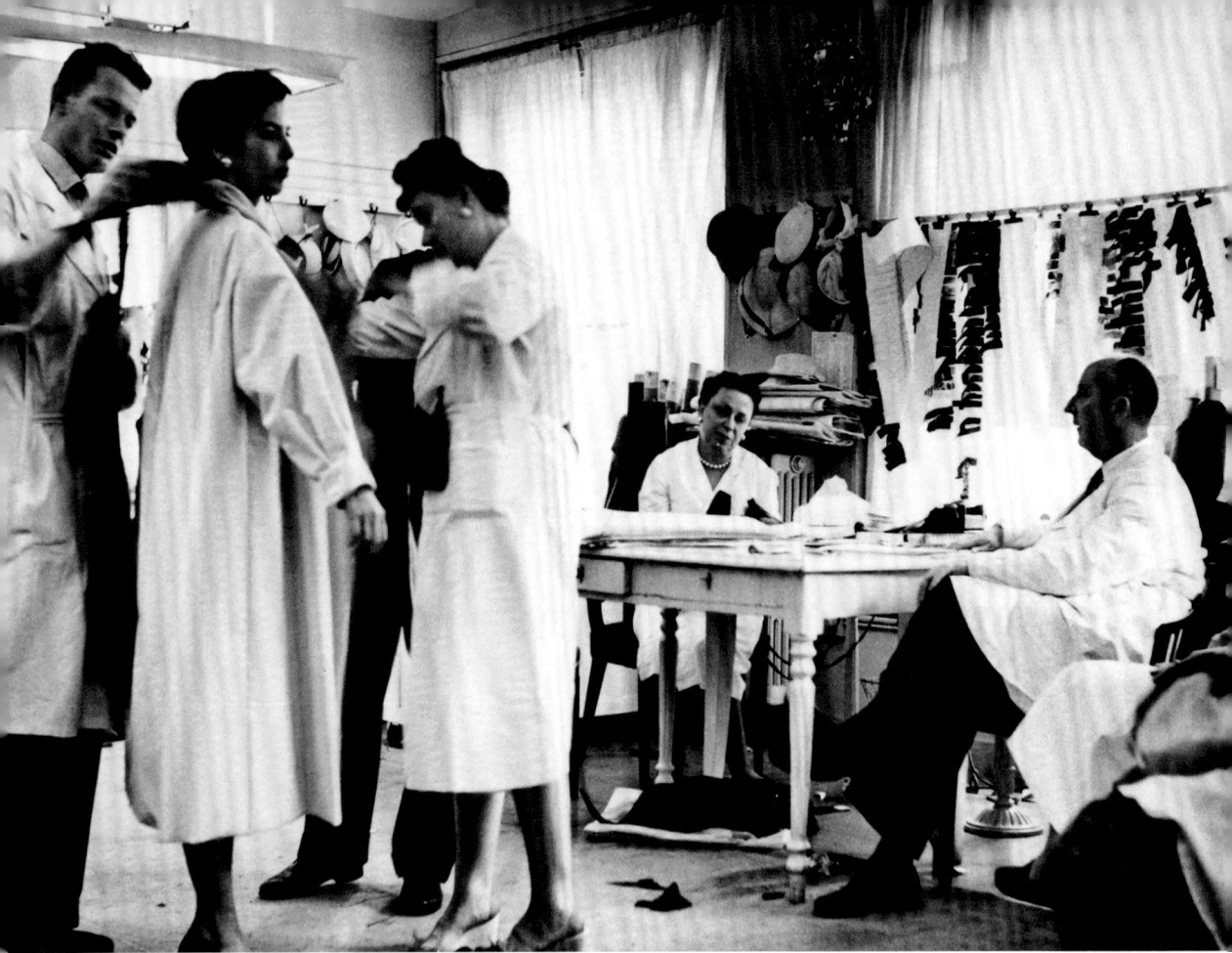

shoulders and fluid, pleated skirts layered with petticoats. Dior reigned supreme for ten years and restored Paris to its title of fashion capital.

The lifelong effort Lagerfeld undertook to reconstruct his past revolved around a central black mark that needed to be concealed: his father's involvement with the Nazis, including membership in various National Socialist organizations to ensure he could stay open for business. After the war, in 1947, the de-Nazification panel concluded that Otto Lagerfeld had aligned with the Nazis out of sheer opportunism, without any ideological conviction, and decided to take no action against the businessman. Still, when nineteen-year-old Karl arrived in Paris in 1952 with his mother, he spun tales of having a Swedish or Danish father. This child of war, emerging from a landscape of ruins, was determined to hide his origins as he embarked upon a new life. He adopted the philosophy of the endless rebeginning, with a singular focus on the present moment—without drawing on the past. "What I show is just a facade," said Lagerfeld. "I owe my truth to no one but myself."[1]

It was there in the French capital, which had once more become the standard of elegance, and where haute couture had entered a second golden age, that Lagerfeld took his first steps as a designer. He gradually began to establish himself in a universe marked by the names of Dior, Jacques

Designer Christian Dior (seated, at right) photographed in his Paris atelier during a fitting session in the early 1950s.

"FASHION IS NEITHER MORAL NOR IMMORAL. IT IS THERE TO LIFT OUR SPIRITS."

—KARL LAGERFELD

KARL LAGERFELD

Left:
Cocktail dress
in cotton poplin
designed by Pierre
Balmain and made by
Zika Ascher, 1957.

Right:
Brigitte Bardot and
Pierre Balmain
during a fitting for
the film *Her Bridal
Night*, July 1956.

Following spread:
Lagerfeld and Yves
Saint Laurent both
receive first prize
at the International
Wool Secretariat
design competition
in Paris in 1954.
Lagerfeld won in
the coat category
and Saint Laurent in
the dress category.
Colette Bracchi won
in the suit category.

Fath, Pierre Balmain, Cristóbal Balenciaga, and Hubert de Givenchy. In 1954, destiny brought together two disparate prodigies who, through their extraordinary creativity, would turn the fashion world upside down: Lagerfeld and Yves Saint Laurent. These two unknowns, who would become like brothers for a time before turning away from each other to reign over rival clans, each won a top prize in a competition organized by the International Wool Secretariat, alongside a third winner, Colette Bracchi. Lagerfeld won in the coat category and Saint Laurent in the dress category, while Bracchi took home the prize in the suit category.

As the story goes, years later, in the company of Saint Laurent and his business partner, Pierre Bergé, Lagerfeld consulted a fortune teller who predicted the career paths of the two budding designers. After prophesying the meteoric rise—and swift end—of Saint Laurent, Lagerfeld was told he would have to wait for his time in the spotlight, but that his reign would begin when the sun had set on his fellow designers. Indeed, what made him so unique was his refusal for years to establish his own fashion house, preferring instead to put his talents at the service of others—even if it meant toiling in the shadows. That allowed him to feed his insatiable appetite as a shape-shifting and secretive creator.

His versatility would soon be on full display as he went to work for Balmain, Jean Patou, Chloé, Fendi, and Chanel. As artistic director, he mixed the DNA of each brand with his own vision, vocabulary, and aesthetic novelties. He was a bibliophile of incredible erudition and a one-man band capable of taking charge from beginning to end, leaving his mark on every step, from sketching to tailoring and staging spectacular shows—not to mention spearheading advertising campaigns, publicity photos, and videos (admittedly, helped by a squad of assistants). He would go on to shape the world of fashion for a full sixty years, striving to make his own life a work of pop culture art, and to disappear behind his legend. "I do not want to be a reality in the lives of others," he once said. "I want to be like an apparition that appears and then disappears."

It would take the pen of a Bossuet and the clairvoyance of Choupette to do complete justice to his life's work. The journey into the world of Lagerfeld proposed by this book reveals the remarkable chapters of fashion history written by this designer in his singular style.

Below:
Fashion creator Lagerfeld at home in Paris in the early 1970s.

Right:
Lagerfeld and his model, receiving first prize in the coat category at the International Wool Secretariat design competition in Paris, 1954.

Following spread, left:
Lily Donaldson photographed by Lagerfeld for the press kit for the fall/winter 2004-2005 haute couture collection.

· Right:
Sketch by Lagerfeld for the Chanel fall/winter 2004-2005 haute couture collection, Chanel archives, Paris.

KARL LAGERFELD

HISTORICAL
CONTEXT

Cars on the Place
de la Concorde,
early 1950s Paris.

By 1952, when Karl Lagerfeld fled a Germany in ruins and made his new home in Paris, determined to enter the closed world of fashion, the city had regained its mantle as the capital of luxury and reaffirmed its place as the cradle of haute couture. The young man who sketched tirelessly and devoured silhouettes suddenly discovered the bohemian freedom of an environment that, after five years of war, had returned to and reinvented French elegance. Gone were the shortages, the scraping by, and the austere, masculine clothes worn by women. The return of peacetime was a hymn to celebration, embodied in the fashion world by Christian Dior. During the Nazi occupation, a few key names had been able to continue their activities in France, such as Cristóbal Balenciaga and Jacques Fath, but many others had closed their doors, including Elsa Schiaparelli, Coco Chanel, Madeleine Vionnet, and Edward Molyneux. After liberation, they reopened in a new world trying to heal its wounds from the war. Creativity and femininity made a comeback, with Dior as one of the primary standard-bearers. After creating the New Look in 1947, he quickly freed himself from it, as he offered a new line and new style every six months. Lines like Corolle, Ailée, Tulipe, H, A, Y, and Flèche secured his fame in France and beyond.

After the war, suspicions hung over the actions of Chanel during the occupation. She was

KARL LAGERFELD

Left:
Kees van Dongen,
Coco Chanel,
circa 1950, private
collection.

Right:
Yves Saint Laurent,
then assistant
designer at Dior,
sketching dresses
and suits.

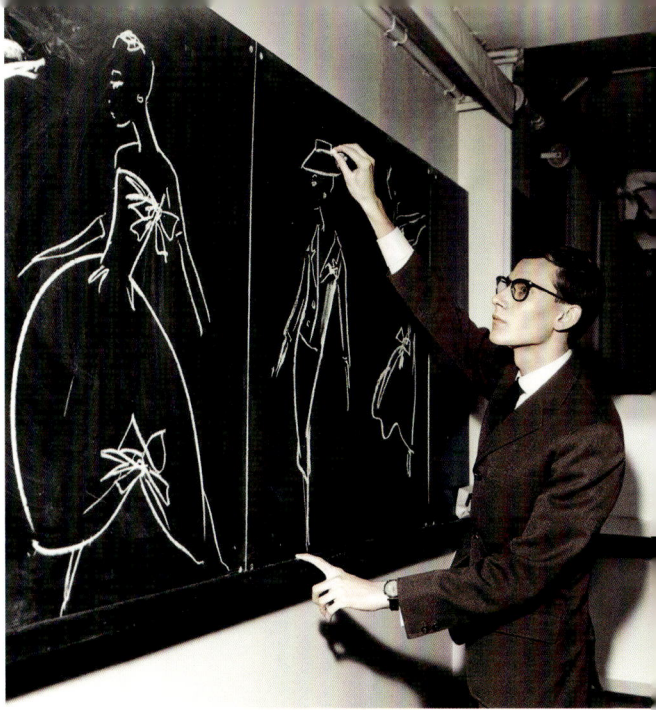

ultimately cleared of wrongdoing, however, and the designer subsequently reopened her shop on Rue Cambon. She continuously jeered Dior for having once again corseted women's bodies, where she had freed them. Chanel had broken from this tradition of corsets and frills as early as the 1920s, emphasizing comfort and freedom of movement in a very basic and real form of emancipation. In 1955, she presented a piece that would become iconic—the tweed suit—as well as her legendary handbag, the 2.55—two jewels that Lagerfeld would frequently reinterpret later on as artistic director for the fashion collections at Chanel.

When Dior died suddenly in 1957, the world of haute couture faltered and went into mourning. Yves Saint Laurent, hired as an assistant at Dior two years earlier, was appointed artistic director. In 1958, he presented his first collection, marked by the Trapèze line, which radically detached itself from the brand's existing aesthetic, going as far as to offer an opposing style: Far from the fitted waist and wasp waist of Dior's New Look, the Trapèze line proposed a soft, fluid silhouette that concealed the body beneath. In pulling from the men's wardrobe for his women's lines, Saint Laurent shook up conventional codes, and the shock was even greater when he brought elements of street fashion into the sphere of haute couture.

Young
Lagerfeld
working
for creator
Jean Patou,
circa 1960.

This was notably the case in 1960 when he turned to the biker jacket for inspiration for his fall/winter collection, with the iconic Chicago jacket made with black crocodile leather.

Meanwhile, during these years of revived opulence and imagination, surrounded by the leading couturiers of the time—including Balenciaga, Fath, Balmain, Louis Féraud, and Hubert de Givenchy, along with his muse, Audrey Hepburn—Lagerfeld immersed himself in everything Paris had to offer. He delved into the party scene, frequenting trendy bars alongside Saint Laurent, Pierre Bergé, and Victoire Doutreleau (Saint Laurent's favorite model and muse to Dior). Saint Laurent, the prince of fashion, rose quickly to prominence. In 1962, he founded his own fashion label with his partner, Bergé, and presented his first haute couture collection under his name. Lagerfeld, meanwhile, got his start in the milieu of haute couture from 1955 to 1958 as an assistant for Balmain, before being appointed artistic director with Jean Patou.

The son of a businessman, Lagerfeld found the idea of opening his own fashion house vulgar, mocking others' desire to attach their name to a brand. He nurtured different aspirations, seeking neither recognition nor the spotlight for himself. A self-taught intellectual, he saw himself as a stylist, a thinker, and an influential actor in the world of

HISTORY

KARL LAGERFELD

Opposite and right:
Fall 1984 ready-to-
wear show, Lagerfeld.

fashion. His art began with concepts, ideas, and sketches before materializing in textiles. Just as he refused to be burdened by his past, he had no desire to be tied down by a fashion house. As he told the *New York Times* in 2002, "It doesn't have to be 'my house, my name, my label, it will die with me.' That's not modern."[2] It was only in 1984 that he finally founded his eponymous label. A truly versatile stylist, he anticipated the trend that would later come to dominate fashion: freelance designers offering their services to established brands. Early on, he described himself as a "hired gun," and he was a very special one at that, particularly gifted at restoring the luster and richness of fading fashion houses.

These struggling labels all saw their fortunes turn around, and in a big way, thanks to the touch of this modern-day King Midas. His judgment was unwavering: haute couture was outdated, and ready-to-wear was the fashion of the future. It was a bold position, but his insight proved to be visionary; long before others, he sensed that the golden age of haute couture was over, and that societal changes, with the rise of consumerism and the expansion of the fashion labels' clientele, would elevate ready-to-wear to new heights. His conception of fashion was rooted in creative innovation for ready-to-wear, which he pushed to its limits before later returning to haute couture—in a revitalized form—infused with a youthful spirit.

INSPIRATION

Inspiration

THE CREATOR'S SOURCES

A man of many facets, Karl Lagerfeld possessed the genius to slip into multiple roles, even embodying the spirit of iconic figures like Coco Chanel to revive a label's essence. While the style of a couturier is often instantly recognizable, and haute couture demands differentiation from other designers, Lagerfeld rewrote the rules. During his years at Balmain, Patou, Chloé, and Fendi, rather than working to create lines that would be easily identifiable to the "in" crowd, he redefined the identity of the labels themselves. Though his audacity and innovations broadly disrupted the luxury industry, he had no desire to be tied to a single look, a fixed visual identity, or even a palette of styles. As fashion journalist Alicia Drake wrote, "Karl resolutely refused to stand for anything; the only thing he accepted as his style constant was the new, the next."[3]

This new approach to fashion was reflected in his unique practice of drawing from a broad and deep pool of sources of inspiration. Lagerfeld described himself as a vampire, a creator who drank up the spirit of the age, capturing its many facets and invisible layers, while also anticipating them. His life and work were marked by multiplicity: a multiplicity of characters crafted over the years, of cultural references, of muses, and of labels.

With fashion designers, it is often straightforward to follow the thread between sources—whether architectural, pictorial, cinematographic, or street-inspired—and the resulting collections. Many, in fact, explicitly reference the influences behind their creations (think Yves Saint Laurent). However, the exercise becomes far more complex with Lagerfeld. His method of combining and crossing a diverse bouquet of inspirations led to creations that frequently obscure their underlying cultural connections. Lagerfeld distanced himself from his own past, yet he drew abundantly from art history, while also tapping into the contemporary world, societal trends, and streetwear—an area where he proved to be one of the keenest observers. In this way, he blended and transformed motifs from painting and artistic tradition, infusing them with elements pulled from underground subcultures.

His dreams were also among the sources of inspiration for the materials, models, cuts, and shapes that feature in his work; as Lagerfeld confided to writers Jean-Christophe Napias and Patrick Mauriès, "Everything good I've ever created I first saw in my dreams. That's why I always keep a drawing pad by my bed."[4] With Lagerfeld, dresses, pants, jackets, and accessories became like books, each offering a

Page 38:
Edvard Munch,
Portrait of Friedrich Nietzsche, circa 1906,
Munch Museet, Oslo.

Page 39:
American rapper
Darryl McDaniels
(aka DMC) from
the hip-hop group
Run-DMC. Concert
at the Greek Theatre,
Los Angeles,
California, June 1987.

Pages 40-41:
Antoine Watteau,
The Shop Sign of Gersaint (detail),
1720, Charlottenburg
Palace, Berlin.

multi-referential, polyphonic text with an original and audacious voice. He could be seen reinserting certain gimmicks from time to time, but he never repeated himself outright, riding a wave of change instead. A dandy and a disciple of Paul Morand's 1941 novel *The Man in a Hurry*, he sought constant renewal, much like a snake shedding its skin over and over again.

During the thirty-six years he spent with Chanel—from 1983 until his death—Lagerfeld left an indelible mark on the fashion world with memorable collections and shows that pushed the boundaries of haute couture and ready-to-wear. For the spring/summer 1991 ready-to-wear collection, he introduced a new look dubbed the "city surfer," while for the fall/winter 1991–1992 ready-to-wear collection, he took inspiration from rappers and hip-hop culture, blending their styles with Chanel's traditional chains and pearls. The insolent energy of the street thus ascended to the catwalk. Lagerfeld dismissed accusations of cultural appropriation flung by those in the rap world—this coalescence was merely part of his aesthetic vampirization, of which he was the ultimate master. His philosophy centered on an intoxicating blend of invention, recycling, cross-references, and street influences. Not only did he achieve a synthesis of the arts, forging dialogues between eras and movements, he also seamlessly merged elements of street fashion with the identities of the fashion houses he served in a rare form of stylistic alchemy.

A superlative scholar and a voracious reader, Lagerfeld placed in his personal pantheon such authors as Emily Dickinson, Jacques-Bénigne Bossuet, Friedrich Hölderlin, Thomas Mann, Else Lasker-Schüler, Roberto Juarroz, Jorge Luis Borges, Racine, Friedrich Nietzsche, Spinoza, Homer, and Louis de Rouvroy, the Duke of Saint-Simon. His favorite books included Stéphane Mallarmé's *Selected Letters*, Rainer Maria Rilke's *The Duino Elegies*, Goethe's *Elective Affinities*, Catherine Pozzi's *Journal*, Madame de La Fayette's *The Princess of Cleves*, *Daphnis and Chloe* by Longus, *The Words* by Jean-Paul Sartre, and *Break of Day* by Colette.[5] In all, his personal library comprised some three hundred thousand volumes. He also collected paintings and furniture, and his broader interests and influences spanned art history, the Age of Enlightenment, and Greco-Roman and Egyptian antiquity, as well as contemporary music, street fashion, and the gay scene. His secret lay in his ability to merge these disparate elements, blending remnants from the past with the ingredients of the present, creating a wholly unique aesthetic.

Fascinated by the eighteenth century and artist Antoine Watteau, Lagerfeld drew inspiration from the painter's compositions for his dresses. His love for the Age of Enlightenment traced back to his childhood, when he had a revelation upon discovering a reproduction of Adolph von Menzel's *Round Table*

"Fashion designers are dictators of taste."
—Karl Lagerfeld

Page 42:
Adolph von Menzel,
Round Table of Frederick II at Sanssouci, 1850,
Sanssouci Palace,
Potsdam, Germany.

Page 43:
Jacques de Bascher
at a costume party.

INSPIRATION

KARL LAGERFELD

INSPIRATION

KARL LAGERFELD

INSPIRATION

KARL LAGERFELD

INSPIRATION

of Frederick II, which depicts Frederick the Great among some of the era's greatest minds, including Voltaire. Surrounded by his own court of extravagant figures and partygoers for whom clothing was a vital form of expression, Lagerfeld found inspiration in his longtime companion, Jacques de Bascher, as well as eccentric personalities like fashion writer Anna Piaggi. Like Andy Warhol, he possessed an extraordinary talent for capturing the spirit of the age, forming an entourage of provocative personalities and flirting with the abyss. That was all the inspiration he needed to endlessly reimagine Piaggi's vintage looks and the splendor of Versailles.

For his Chanel spring/summer 2019 haute couture collection, Lagerfeld reimagined the Chanel woman through the lens of Madame de Pompadour, the famed mistress of Louis XV—a source of inspiration he had already explored during his time at Chloé in the 1970s. The collection featured ruffled dresses, boat necks, and multi-fold skirts, drawing from his beloved eighteenth century, the era of merchants and mercers who supplied the aristocracy with luxurious finery. The spirit of the Enlightenment intertwined with the monarchical splendor of Versailles as Lagerfeld celebrated the French taste that reigned over the court and the house of Bourbon. Embroidered flower-patterned motifs, crafted by the Atelier Lesage, adorned the designs, while feathers accentuated the floral silhouettes. Inspired by lingerie and eighteenth-century wardrobes, the dresses were infused with a light, youthful energy, combining the volumes of bell or sheath skirts with jackets featuring a double-breasted detail that added a rebellious, rock-inspired edge.

The collections Lagerfeld designed for Chanel symbolize the multiplicity of his inspirations, whether weaving a common thread or braiding diverse influences together. It's worth taking a closer look at a few standout moments. The Chanel spring/summer 1985 haute couture collection blends an homage to Watteau with Chanel's signature aesthetic, echoing the artist's painting Pierrot—featuring the commedia dell'arte character of the same name—and presenting opulent eighteenth-century-inspired embroidered dresses, including a sumptuous design based on the character Colombine, worn by model Jerry Hall. The splendor of Versailles illuminates the fall/winter 1987–1988 haute couture collection, drawing inspiration from Jean-Baptiste Lully's opera Atys. Renaissance influences then take center stage in the fall/winter 1988–1989 haute couture collection, which Lagerfeld dedicated to the Elizabethan era. Shakespeare's presence looms large over the runway, with each look bearing the name of one of his characters. The show closes with Ophelia dressed in a wedding gown.

Other notable sources of inspiration, as previously mentioned, include California surfers in the spring/summer 1991 ready-to-wear collection; the rap scene aesthetic (fall/winter 1991–1992

Page 46:
Surfer deep inside the barrel of a breaking wave.

Page 47:
Maurice Quentin de La Tour, *Portrait of the Marquise de Pompadour*, 1755, Louvre Museum, Paris.

Page 48:
Jackson Pollock, *Number 16*, 1949, private collection.

ready-to-wear); and the extravagant hippie spirit of the 1960s, described by *Women's Wear Daily* as a fusion of Janis Joplin and Jackson Pollock (fall/winter 1992–1993 haute couture). Hairstyles inspired by seventeenth-century fontange headdresses, reimagined with lace and a punk edge, featured prominently in the spring/summer 1996 haute couture collection, while equestrianism defined the spring/summer 1997 ready-to-wear line. Other influences that enriched Lagerfeld's Chanel collections include the flappers of the Roaring Twenties and French designer Paul Poiret (spring/summer 1998 haute couture); Japanese culture and Zen Buddhism (fall/winter 1998–1999 haute couture); and the Orient and ancient China, blending Chinese styles with touches of 1930s Hollywood glamour (*Métiers d'Art Paris-Shanghai*, 2009–2010).

Cinema and literature also made their mark: the film *Last Year at Marienbad* by Alain Resnais, for which Chanel herself designed the costumes, infused the spring/summer 2011 ready-to-wear collection; James Dean and the costumes of *Rebel Without a Cause* left their imprint on the spring/summer 1996 ready-to-wear collection; a year later, it was a unique Nordic cocktail where knights, Hans Christian Andersen's fairy tales, and Ingmar Bergman's films mingled with Danish author Karen Blixen and Henrik Ibsen's *Hedda Gabler* (fall/winter 1997–1998 haute couture); and in 2009, it was an eclectic bouquet of the Venice Carnival, Giacomo Casanova, the Lido, the Thomas Mann book and Luchino Visconti film *Death in Venice*, and Marchesa Luisa Casati (Venice cruise, 2009–2010). Lagerfeld was also influenced by the French New Wave.

Painting and the art world, too, provide the backdrop for several collections: Jean-Honoré Fragonard's country paintings and Marie-Antoinette's hamlet at the Palace of Versailles (spring/summer 2010 ready-to-wear); the Gothic universe through the lens of artist Anselm Kiefer, painter Caspar David Friedrich, and filmmaker Fritz Lang, in a postapocalyptic atmosphere (fall/winter 2011–2012 ready-to-wear); and the pop art movement with Roy Lichtenstein (fall/winter 2001–2002 ready-to-wear).

Lagerfeld also turned to exceptional figures to set the tone for many of his collections: British writer Nancy Cunard, a political activist with a strikingly unconventional style, is in the spotlight in the spring/summer 1989 haute couture collection; Suzy Parker, a famous American model and actress in the 1950s, was honored in the spring/summer 1995 haute couture collection; and Empress Sisi and the splendors of the Austro-Hungarian Empire under the Habsburgs were at the fore in the *Métiers d'Art Paris-Salzburg* 2014–2015 collection. Other prominent influences included the dandyism of Englishman Beau Brummell (the *Belle Brummelle* collection, fall/winter 2009–2010 ready-to-wear); Mary, Queen of Scots (*Métiers d'Art*

Page 49:
American singer Janis Joplin on stage, late 1960s.

Page 50:
Actress Louise Brooks in a satin dress, 1928.

Page 51:
Kusakabe Kimbei, *Japanese Toilet*, circa 1880.

INSPIRATION

KARL LAGERFELD

INSPIRATION

KARL LAGERFELD

INSPIRATION

703-89

KARL LAGERFELD

INSPIRATION

Paris-Edinburgh, 2012–2013); French painter Marie Laurencin (spring/summer 2011 haute couture), and dancer/choreographer Isadora Duncan.

In the case of Lagerfeld, no list of interests and influences could ever be truly exhaustive, but to paint as clear of a picture as possible, it is also worth citing classical dance, the world of sports, bikers, surfing, rock 'n' roll, Hollywood's golden age glamour and femmes fatales, the cosmos, the astral world, organ music, Russian culture (folklore, Imperial Russia, the Russian avant-garde, constructivism), 3D pop-up books, the Byzantine Empire and its mosaics, the Egypt of the pharaohs, ancient Greece, the underwater world, the secret world of crystals, the wind, nature, forests, India, German Romanticism, the Wild West, digital technology, Latin and Cuban culture . . .

The visual stimuli of street fashion fueled Lagerfeld's audacity. He was the first to introduce tennis shoes into haute couture collections, bringing sneakers to the catwalks as early as 1976 with Chloé. Unlike Dior, Yves Saint Laurent, Balenciaga, Paco Rabanne, or Thierry Mugler, Lagerfeld left behind not a style but a spirit. A style can confine, petrify, or clip one's wings. Taking over the artistic direction of a prestigious house like Chanel could easily paralyze, intimidate, and instill the fear of betraying its heritage. Lagerfeld, however, refused to be crushed by the weight of Chanel's tradition. Instead, he preserved its spirit and essence while shaking up its codes.

Lagerfeld's intent was to make Chanel roll over in her grave so that, as he put it, she might seem alive again. And in so doing, he redefined haute couture. Lagerfeld understood that a luxury brand spanning haute couture, ready-to-wear, accessories, and perfumes had to open itself up to street culture, social movements, and avant-garde artistry. Better than anyone else, he was able to size up the zeitgeist, capturing the most salient traits of the time and the renewal of social mores that were underway. As the rhythm of change accelerated over the decades, he imposed on fashion—and on himself—a perpetual renewal, to always stay aligned with, or ahead of, his era. In the 1980s, for example, he offered oversize shoulders that perfectly reflected the bold, exaggerated style of the period. "Starting in the 1950s and staying on the pulse each ensuing decade—that's incredible," observed art dealer Philippe Garner. "Most designers had their moment of glory, usually lasting no more than a decade, with a vision that corresponded to a particular era. But Karl's vision was unique, reflecting his own uniqueness: As the times changed, so did Lagerfeld's perspective."[6]

His designs were rooted in rhetoric and a mastery of pictorial composition. A devoted reader of Jacques-Bénigne Bossuet, Saint-Simon, Louis Aragon, and Michel Houellebecq, he approached fashion as a game of shapes, colors, materials, and

Page 54:
Decorative murals with motifs from ancient Egypt. Hand-finished chromolithograph by Antoine Pralon, based on *L'Ornement polychrome* by Albert Racinet (Firmin Didot, Paris, 1869-73).

Page 55:
El Lissitzky, *Untitled*, circa 1919-20, Peggy Guggenheim Collection, Venice.

Page 56:
Statue of Antinous, made from Parian marble, found near the Temple of Apollo in Delphi.

cuts, all of it orchestrated through myriad stylistic devices—a constantly evolving aesthetic palette. In the fashion world, he introduced the visual equivalent of Bossuet's *Funeral Orations*, matching its eloquence and replacing its solemnity with celebrations of life and joy.

CLASSICISM

What is often referred to as Karl Lagerfeld's "classicism" reflects his fascination with certain artistic and historical periods of particular richness that continuously nourished his creations: Egyptian, Greek, and Roman antiquity, the court of Versailles, and the Aufklärung (Enlightenment). Among the fashion world's most frequently recurring sources of inspiration for haute couture is ancient Greece—that is to say, a fantasized, idealized version of it reimagined by couturiers. From the iconic 1951 photo shoot at the Acropolis, where Christian Dior unveiled his locally inspired haute couture dresses, to the Chanel 2017–2018 cruise collection by Lagerfeld (*La Modernité de l'Antiquité*) and Dior's own 2022 cruise collection in Athens under the direction of Maria Grazia Chiuri, Greece has long captivated designers. In 2019, Dolce & Gabbana even held a haute couture show at a Greek temple in Agrigento, Sicily. For Lagerfeld, Greece, ancient Rome, and the Egypt of the pharaohs enriched his creative universe in myriad ways, as he updated and reinterpreted the aesthetic codes of antiquity. Pleats, draping, togas, flowing sleeves, the peplos (a folded garment for women), Spartan sandals, and white-and-gold jewelry—these elements formed a complete design vocabulary rooted in the ancient world, offering a vast reservoir of shapes, styles, and patterns that Lagerfeld seamlessly integrated into his work.

This return to our roots, this bridge between Greece, the cradle of Western civilization, and our contemporary era, can take many forms. Sometimes it is a simple cruise through time, where the seeker simply chisels away on the surface with the aim of extracting certain elements from the classical aesthetic codes. This aligns with fashion's perpetual tendency to rewrite the past in the present, a form of retrospective that represents a philosophy of revival; in this way, it allows for reflection on the modern as well. We strip the old to dress the new. Greek fashion thus becomes one vein to explore among many, each intertwined in a web of pop creation. But it can also be more than that. The return to Hellenic culture can be indicative of more profound inspiration—a heady, burning passion for Greek mythology, philosophy, architecture,

Page 57:
Detail of an embroidered panel, queen's chambers, Palace of Versailles.

Page 58:
View of the Milky Way.

Page 59:
Contrast of blue and white, Santorini Island, Greece.

"An idea without execution is a dream."
—Louis de Rouvroy, Duke of Saint-Simon

INSPIRATION

KARL LAGERFELD

INSPIRATION

KARL LAGERFELD

INSPIRATION

and thought. This was true for both Coco Chanel and Lagerfeld. For Lagerfeld, his cross-referencing was not part of some superficial "new antique" trend intent on merely copying and pasting antiquity for modern audiences. Instead, it reflected an unwavering fascination with a civilization that continues to shape the imagination of designers and their vision of the world.

The ancient Greece that Lagerfeld put forward for Chanel, particularly in the 2017–2018 cruise collection, *La Modernité de l'Antiquité*, straddled the bygone past and its glorious heritage, and emphasized its grandeur and freedom. "For me, Greece is the cradle of beauty and culture," he explained. "There was a wonderful liberty of movement that has since disappeared. The Greeks had something that has been lost—the body was not something that was hidden, that you had to be ashamed of as it turned out to be in later centuries . . . Reality is of no interest to me. I use what I like. My Greece is an idea." It is both a lost world—a submerged Atlantis to which Lagerfeld payed homage—and a civilizational space whose cultural richness has endured through time.

Even though he claimed not to cultivate nostalgia, Lagerfeld's words and designs do reveal a hint of melancholy—a longing for a vanished Eden, a golden age forever lost. What leaps from the fifth and fourth centuries BCE into the twenty-first century, shepherded by the designer, are the flowing dresses and draping, the embroidered tunics, the tiaras, the gleaming jewels, and the aesthetic codes of Greek beauty, to be repurposed for post-Greek goddesses. There are prints evoking laurel wreaths and pleats echoing Greek columns; there is an entire vision of the Mediterranean informed by Helen of Troy, aristocratic elegance, classical statuary, the brilliance of pristine marble, and the forms of Doric, Ionic, and Corinthian capitals. What transcends time are the magnified bodies, the golden ratio, and the women of all stripes: muses, priestesses, pastoral and majestic figures, even incarnations of Venus and Artemis.

For Lagerfeld, as he often emphasized, Greek classicism exemplified the timelessness of the measures of beauty. They are not merely a cultural construct tied to a specific era or society; if ancient Greece, the cradle of our culture, feels more modern even than the present day, it is precisely because it has bequeathed to us a visual grammar of beauty that *transcends* time. Revived by the Renaissance, these ideals continue to shape our understanding of aesthetics across the past, present, and future. This underscores the notion that fashion is a form of reminiscence, but also of politics, reflecting a subjective, active engagement with history.

Lagerfeld's canonization of the Greek dawn implied that we ourselves live in a twilight era. But

Page 62:
Statues of Ramses II, entrance to the Great Temple at Abu Simbel, Egypt.

Page 63:
Botanical plate of camellias, illustrated by Augusta Innes Withers, circa 1840.

Page 64:
Detail of the colorful plumage of a peacock.

Page 65:
Gold bracelet from the tomb of Amenemope, mounted with a scarab made of lapis lazuli that bears the gold sun disk.

The tubular bracelet
is set with carnelian
and other semi-
precious stones. On
the back, cartouches
bear the royal names
of the pharaoh's
predecessor,
Psusennes I. Third
Intermediate Period,
Twenty-First
Dynasty, 993-984
BCE, Tanis, Egypt.

Pages 66-67:
Anna Wintour (far
left), Lagerfeld, and
Linda Evangelista,
fitting session
for the Fall 1993
couture collection,
Chanel atelier,
Paris, July 1993.

for the Greek deities, too, they gain a renewed exis-tence as they grace the catwalks and breathe fresh life into the world of today. History occasionally expe-riences air currents that disrupt the natural processes of forgetting and waning, allowing the past to reso-nate sharply in the fabric of the present. Lagerfeld had only to extend a simple invitation to the divinities of Olympus for the ancients to bring their weight to bear on the here and now and permeate contempo-rary society. Some may have been weary from their long slumber, but Lagerfeld awakened them with his deft touch and invited them to feast at the banquet of the twentieth and twenty-first centuries. His designs brimmed with playful nods, including references to the Spartan wardrobe (his flowing linen dresses) and the goddess Athena, whose symbol—the owl—adorns a minaudière. During the show, DJ Michel Gaubert's soundtrack seamlessly blended the avant-garde compositions of Iannis Xenakis with the progressive rock of Aphrodite's Child, infusing the moment with an atmosphere that bridged antiquity and modernity.

For his *Métiers d'Art Paris-New York* 2018–2019 collection, Lagerfeld selected the Temple of Dendur at the Metropolitan Museum of Art as the stage for his journey to the land of the pharaohs. Rescued from the rising waters of the Nile during the construction of the Aswan Dam and reassembled at the museum, this temple dedicated to Isis provided the perfect backdrop for a vibrant homage to ancient Egypt, spotlighting its polytheism, its worship of the sun god, and its reverence for gold (a passion shared by Chanel). The collection seamlessly blended Chanel's signature elements with Egyptian motifs, featuring camellias, sequins, the iconic double-C logo, embroidered flowers on white dresses, beetle-inspired accents, gold-hued tights, ornate pectoral ornaments, and richly textured tweeds—all imbued with the light of the sun and infused with golden energy.

In this homage to ancient Egypt, transporting us to the banks of the Nile, a glamorous touch of modernity intertwined with a Hollywood atmosphere, evoking memories of Elizabeth Taylor in 1963's *Cleopatra*. The traditional Usekh collar, once worn by people of high rank, was reimagined in the form of ultra-modern amulet collars and ornate breastplates, while gold-rich ensembles paid tribute to Ra, the falcon-headed sun god and creator of the universe. The collection's Egyptomania further came to life through golden shoes crafted by Massaro, accor-dion pleats in black tulle and organza, and tweeds adorned with hand-painted gold ribbons. Lagerfeld masterfully complemented the hieroglyphs of the Egyptian Empire with the symbols of the twenty-first century, forging a dialogue with the long-lost pha-raohs and building bridges across millennia.

KARL LAGERFELD

INSPIRATION

KARL LAGERFELD

INSPIRATION

KARL LAGERFELD

INSPIRATION

HIS MUSES

The looks that Karl Lagerfeld crafted were embodied by muses who often played multiple roles—at once sources of inspiration, faces of the brand, and representatives of the particular elegance of the era. As with all things, Lagerfeld embraced a medley of muses. Rather than limiting himself to a single figure, he chose a constellation of models whose beauty was meant to be iconic and reflective of their time. Alongside figures in his entourage like Jacques de Bascher and the eccentric Anna Piaggi, who inspired him in their own way, a select group of models were tasked with embodying the essence of the Chanel woman, the Chloé woman, or the Lagerfeld woman, including Ines de la Fressange, Claudia Schiffer, Vanessa Paradis, Carla Bruni, Pat Cleveland, Linda Evangelista, Kate Moss, Stella Tennant, Cara Delevingne, Lily-Rose Depp, and Kaia Gerber.

Lagerfeld's ascent in the 1980s coincided with the rise of the supermodel, against the backdrop of an increasingly globalized industry that was undergoing consolidation, bankrolled by luxury conglomerates, and where powerful multinational corporations held sway. From that point on, the fashion world was subsumed by a logic of balance sheets and profitability, and swept up in the commodification of cultural goods, creative works, and even individuals. As the crown jewel of neoliberalism, the luxury sector lost much of its freedom and spontaneity. The era of superstar models then began to decline in the mid-1990s, eclipsed by the rise of minimalist and grunge trends, only to resurface in the 2000s and rise to prominence once more.

Anointed by Lagerfeld in 1979 during his tenure at Chloé, de la Fressange came to define a new image of elegance as the archetype of the modern Parisian woman. Captivated by her ultra-slim figure, narrow hips, natural chic, short brown hair, and aristocratic manner and pedigree—as well as her resemblance to Coco Chanel—Lagerfeld made her the face of Chanel from 1983 to 1989. But her collaboration with Lagerfeld ended abruptly when she accepted to be the model for the bust of national French symbol Marianne—a move he disapproved of. De la Fressange, who had personified the Chanel woman of the 1980s—expressing, through her aura, body, and freedom of style, what Lagerfeld referred to as the "Chanel idea"—finally reconciled with the designer more than two decades later. She took to the runway for Chanel in 2010 for the spring/summer 2011 ready-to-wear show.

After his breakup with de la Fressange, Lagerfeld made a dramatic shift. His brand of fashion existed on the bleeding edge, and that required his muses to change with the times. Blonde, perfectly proportioned, with a striking resemblance to Brigitte

Page 70:
Anna Piaggi, Milan,
September 2010.

Page 71:
Baptiste Giabiconi,
Chanel spring/
summer 2016 haute
couture show, Paris
Fashion Week,
January 2016.

Page 72:
Ines de la Fressange,
Fendi fashion
show, fall 1984.

Bardot, Schiffer became the new Chanel frontwoman. In an interview with *Le Monde*, Lagerfeld went as far as to say, "If I had to fight in the Trojan War, Claudia would be my Hélène." As with her predecessor, Schiffer and Lagerfeld eventually had a falling out, before later reconciling. As eras now come to an end faster than during the Trojan War, Lagerfeld continued to cycle through his muses and brand ambassadors regularly. There was Kristen McMenamy, with her unconventional beauty; Tennant, who embodied an androgynous, gender-fluid aesthetic; the doe-eyed beauty of Paradis; Delevingne, with her untamed, natural energy; and model and media personality Kendall Jenner, whose glamorous yet effortless beauty personifies Generation Z.

In essayist and critic Roland Barthes's analysis, fashion is a system of signs, a semiotic empire that flows through the bodies of models—angelic intermediaries who serve to accentuate the magnificence of the clothes.[7] Placed within a framework where image, imagination, symbolism, desire, and fantasy are forced to contend with consumerism and the entertainment industry, Lagerfeld's models embody the mythology of the contemporary world. As crystallizations of Lagerfeld's vision of beauty, figures like de la Fressange, Schiffer, and Baptiste Giabiconi—along with, more fleetingly, Naomi Campbell, Julianne Moore, Tilda Swinton, Rihanna, Willow Smith, and others—exist at the threshold between reality and dreams.

A true Proustian character, Jacques de Bascher[8] was Lagerfeld's greatest love and Yves Saint Laurent's destructive paramour. Fascinated by decadence, fin-de-siècle literature, and Joris-Karl Huysmans's *À rebours*, with its eccentric protagonist, Jean des Esseintes, this prince of the night embodied dark dandyism, submerging himself in leather-clad orgies and cocaine-fueled hedonism, tinged with the melancholy of a lost paradise. Drawn to the abyss, he navigated both the seedy slums and the haut monde. A son of provincial nobility obsessed with his aristocratic origins and the scent of old France, de Bascher defied societal norms with audacious flair.

He was a consummate aesthete seeking dark thrills, and he orchestrated a series of unforgettable soirées—among them, the "Black Moratorium" party held in honor of Lagerfeld during Paris Fashion Week at a disco called La Main Bleue. The invitation read, "Xavier de Castella and Jacques de Bascher request the joy and pleasure of your company all night long from October 24 to 25, 1977, for a Black Moratorium evening in honor of Karl Lagerfeld (black tragic dress absolutely mandatory)." In a signature moment of elegance and wit, de Bascher once summed up his life and his bond with Lagerfeld by saying, "People think I don't work, but I do—I inspire Karl."

On the subject of his muse and socialite companion, who embraced sex, drugs, and sartorial elegance as a way of life, Lagerfeld confided to

Page 73:
Jerry Hall, Chanel fashion show, spring 1985.

Page 74:
Naomi Campbell, Chloé spring/ summer 1994 ready-to-wear show.

Page 75:
Claudia Schiffer, fall/ winter 1995-1996 ready-to-wear collection, Lagerfeld, Paris Fashion Week, March 1995.

INSPIRATION

KARL LAGERFELD

INSPIRATION

KARL LAGERFELD

INSPIRATION

KARL LAGERFELD

INSPIRATION

journalist Marie Ottavi, "Jacques de Bascher, when he was young, was a devil with Garbo's face . . . . He didn't dress like anyone; he was ahead of everyone. He made me laugh more than anyone. He was the opposite of me. He was also impossible and despicable. He was perfect. He sparked incredible cases of jealousy." A free spirit of the 1970s and 1980s, de Bascher was always in search of incendiary pleasures and debauchery. He roamed snobbish parties, backrooms, Club Sept, and Le Palace. A disciple of Dorian Gray and a prince of style with an innate talent for finding just the right look, he was also a consummate seducer. He celebrated his engagement to Diane de Beauvau-Craon[9] in Rome with great pomp and splendor. They never married, but she remained his partner in escapades, embracing decadence as he did as an aesthetic philosophy. For de Bascher, happiness was chemical and relied on the art of style. Erudite, hedonistic, and drawn by chaos, he sought extreme experiences and liminal spaces, all framed by a philosophy of frivolity. His personal journey was part indulgence, part crucifixion.

Bascher died of complications due to AIDS in 1989. When Lagerfeld bought a home near Hamburg in 1991, he named it "Villa Jako" in his honor, and in 1998, he launched a new men's fragrance called Jako. An avid reader of Emily Dickinson, Lagerfeld might have thought of his companion when considering the line "You cannot solder an Abyss / With Air."[10] Similarly, as he read the *Memoirs* of the Duke of Saint-Simon, one sentence surely brought de Bascher to mind: "One had to make an effort to stop looking at him."

Since their meeting in Paris in 1973, Piaggi—the eccentric fashion columnist known for her whimsical outfits and vast cultural knowledge—maintained a close relationship with Lagerfeld. As editor in chief of *Vogue Italia* for over twenty years, and as a journalist for *Panorama* and *Arianna*, she also led the avant-garde Italian magazine *Vanity* (illustrated by Antonio Lopez), where she unraveled the mysteries of fashion and earned the status of a muse. Renowned for her audacious combinations of styles and her collection of extravagant hats, often created by milliner Stephen Jones, Piaggi transformed her daily wardrobe into a kind of performance art. Her life itself would become a work of art, a continuous invention of wildly free looks, forming an extraordinary reservoir of ideas from which Lagerfeld in particular drew inspiration.

In *Anna Chronique*,[11] Lagerfeld explores her persona through a collection of more than two hundred illustrations. In watercolors, pencil, and ink, he composes a kind of fashion diary chronicling the stylistic brilliance of Piaggi, celebrated as a queen of vintage and eclectic looks. Of Karl, Piaggi once said, "He doesn't just pin a piece of cloth on a model; he captures the spirit of taste."[12] In the vast library of the world, with all its resources and sources of inspiration, Lagerfeld—a self-taught genius who described

Page 78: Lagerfeld at a soirée at Le Palace, Paris.

Page 79: Lagerfeld and Anna Piaggi at one of the legendary parties at Le Palace.

Pages 80-81: Lagerfeld aside a portrait of Choupette at the opening of her photo exhibition in Berlin, February 3, 2015.

himself as "a total improvisation"—trusted his intuition. He deconstructed, reworked, and reassembled ideas to create designs that were as inventive as they were instinctive.

Finally, there is the microcosm of friends who gravitated around Lagerfeld in Paris. The princes and princesses of Club Sept, Le Palace, and the famous brasserie La Coupole formed a nebula of muses who nourished his creations, including the small band from the United States—Corey Tippin, Lopez, Juan Ramos, Cleveland, Donna Jordan—but also Victoire de Castellane, as well as many from Saint Laurent's own inner circle, such as Loulou de La Falaise, Thadée Klossowski de Rola, Paloma Picasso, and Clara Saint.

CHOUPETTE

How does a cat become a muse, an inexhaustible source of inspiration, and an international icon? In 2011, Choupette, a charming three-month-old snow-white Burmese cat with "starry sapphire blue" eyes (as described by Karl Lagerfeld), entered the designer's life. Originally belonging to model Baptiste Giabiconi, the feline was initially left with Lagerfeld for a short time in Giabiconi's absence. The Kaiser promptly fell in love with her, and she ended up staying with him, becoming Princess Choupette in the process. Choupette's elegance and sophistication, her whims, her "royal gait" (again, according to Lagerfeld), her natural beauty—every bit of her was an aesthetic revelation and a source of endless inspiration. She was the catalyst for countless ideas, designs, and looks. She graced magazine covers; posed with Linda Evangelista, Laetitia Casta, and Kendall Jenner; inspired a photography book by Lagerfeld; and even contributed to a Shu Uemura makeup capsule collection, where the eyeshadow was an homage to her sapphire-blue eyes. And her influence and standing only grew from there. The blue hues of Chanel's spring/summer 2012 haute couture collection also drew inspiration from the color of her eyes, and subsequent lines of accessories paid tribute to her as well, including handbags with cat-head motifs.

Marcel Proust's character Swann is known for associating the women he loves with paintings and works of art, and Lagerfeld did likewise with Choupette, whom he saw as a kindred spirit to the Infanta Margaret Theresa in Velázquez's painting *Las Meninas*. His adoration for her was absolute. In modern French literature, cats have been given a special place by such notable figures as Jean Cocteau, Colette, and Paul Léautaud. Now, Choupette has become a modern-day muse in her own right.

"She is the center of my world. She is kind of Greta Garbo. There is something unforgettable about her, the way she moves. She's an inspiration for elegance. For attitude."
—Karl Lagerfeld on his cat, Choupette

Page 82:
Lagerfeld drawing at his Paris studio, spring 1979.

Page 83:
The designer appears alongside the models at the end of the Chanel spring/summer 2004 ready-to-wear show, October 2003.

KARL LAGERFELD

INSPIRATION

KARL LAGERFELD

INSPIRATION

KARL LAGERFELD

INSPIRATION

BEHIND THE SCENES

Behind-The-Scenes

LAGERFELD BEFORE LAGERFELD

KARL LAGERFELD

Lagerfeld at
Jean Patou, fitting
session for a model,
Paris, 1958.

After winning the coat prize in a competition organized by the International Wool Secretariat, Karl Lagerfeld began his career at Balmain in 1955, joining the fashion house as an assistant. Founded in 1945 at 44 Rue François Premier in Paris, Balmain was renowned for its sober style, offering dresses and suits in dark or muted tones, with a strong emphasis on embroidery and an architectural approach to design. Founder Pierre Balmain embodied a quintessential French elegance, distinct from the avant-garde spirit of the time. American writer Alice B. Toklas once described it as a "new French style."

At Balmain, Lagerfeld learned his craft hands-on, contributing to notable creations like the wedding dress worn by Brigitte Bardot in *Her Bridal Night*. But he found the house's lack of boldness and modernity stifling. Reflecting on his time there from 1955 to 1962, Lagerfeld described it as a rather bitter experience, citing a horrible atmosphere, harsh working conditions, and low wages for the seamstresses. Despite all of this, his time at Balmain was formative, helping him hone his extraordinary visual memory and develop his talent for archival research, skills that would enable him to sketch an entire collection from memory or trace the stylistic evolution of Christian Dior.

In 1958, following the departure of Marc Bohan, Lagerfeld was appointed artistic director

KARL LAGERFELD

at Jean Patou—a brand still cloaked in prestige but whose luster had faded since the death of its founder in 1936. It was within this constraining environment that the young designer debuted his first collection, the Ligne K. While it was well-received for its freshness and tasteful elegance, it failed to break through. A sharp observer of the shifts reshaping both fashion and society, Lagerfeld sensed that the future lay in ready-to-wear. He viewed haute couture as trapped in a declining world—burdened by its heritage, economically fragile, and accessible only to a small elite.

After discreetly departing from Patou in 1963, and uninterested in founding his own fashion house, Lagerfeld became an independent designer, channeling his extraordinary creativity to revitalize the identities of various labels. As author Patrick Mauriès writes in his introduction to *Chanel: Défilés*, for Lagerfeld, these brands were like "a succession of masks, or identities. He achieved the extraordinary feat—which was counter to the very system and logic of fashion—of being a designer content to simply lend his signature . . . He was the man of all brands and the brand of none, except himself."[13] Foreseeing the shift in the fashion industry that would propel ready-to-wear into the realm of luxury, Lagerfeld bid farewell to haute couture. He only returned to it two decades later,

KARL LAGERFELD

Left page:
Lagerfeld with a
model, early 1960s.

Below:
Lagerfeld presenting
his fall/winter 1969
collection for Chloé.

at Chanel, where he would write some of the most celebrated chapters of his career.

Lagerfeld was prolific and relentlessly hardworking, and once he was gone from Patou, he began to create not only clothing but also accessories, shoes, and brooches for an array of brands including Repetto, Mario Valentino, Krizia, Tiziani, Max Mara, and Charles Jourdan. By the 1960s, ready-to-wear clothing, once broadly denigrated by the French for being mass-produced, was gaining prestige and carving out its place in the fashion scene. A true visionary, Lagerfeld perceived before anyone else the societal shift underway. He saw that the fashion world was about to have its own revolution, not so unlike that of 1789, that would bring down the old hierarchical structure of haute couture, dethrone its aristocratic dominance, and redefine its codes. The first seeds of this transformation were planted in 1957, when Lagerfeld discovered the fashion house Chloé, founded by Gaby Aghion, at one of its fashion shows. This would ultimately lead to his joining their design studio six years later, for the fall/winter 1964–1965 collection. This marked the beginning of a lengthy collaboration, with Lagerfeld soon taking the helm as the house's creative director.

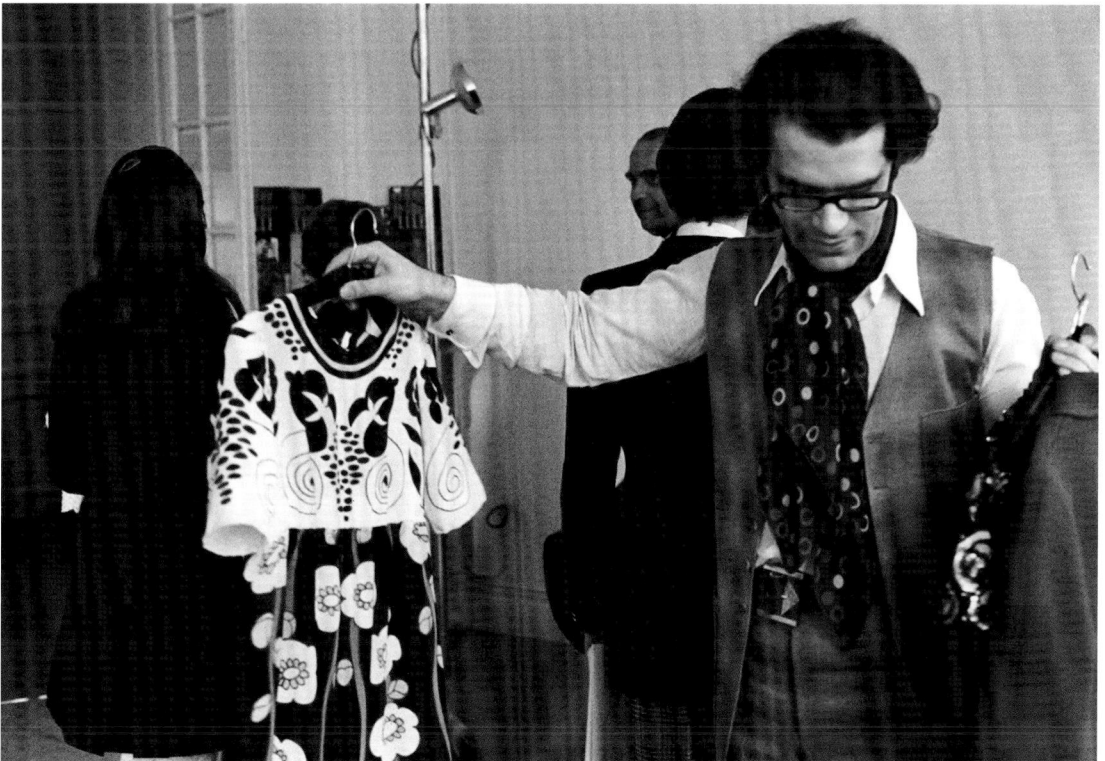

THE CHLOÉ AND
FENDI YEARS

Left page:
Models wearing the
"Bain" and "Brise"
("Bath" and "Breeze")
in embroidered silk
crepe, designed by
Lagerfeld, Chloé
fall/winter 1983
ready-to-wear show.

Following spread:
Fendi fashion show,
spring 1983.

In step with the liberation of both fashion and societal norms in the 1960s and 1970s, Chloé embraced a kind of bohemian chic, a romantic aesthetic characterized by fluid silhouettes and fabrics. A pioneer in ready-to-wear, the house's founder, Gaby Aghion (born Gabrielle Hanoka), worked with her partner, Jacques Lenoir, to introduce a relaxed and light fashion sensibility that broke away from the stiff formality and rigid structure of earlier styles. Their use of embroidery, silk crepe, lace, and a palette of pinks and beiges—evoking Aghion's Egyptian heritage—was an ode to color and movement. With his signature touch, Lagerfeld infused the brand with fresh energy, creating lighter coats, pairing ethereal dresses with tennis shoes, and designing long, light skirts and airy blouses.

His musical ear, acute senses, and ability to immerse himself in the creative universes of others allowed Lagerfeld to not only renew the spirit of Chloé but bring similar success to Fendi and Chanel later on. Lagerfeld captured and internalized every nuance and layer of each brand in a kind of symbiosis that allowed him to both honor and reinvent their identities. It was a process rooted in his pursuit of a quintessence, aligned with the broader zeitgeist, combined with an artful interpretation and reimagining of each house's signature.

BEHIND-THE-SCENES

KARL LAGERFELD

The references that inspired Lagerfeld for his Chloé collections were drawn from his vast bank of cultural knowledge, spanning all the arts, with a special focus on cinema. He stayed with them for nearly two decades, from 1964 to 1983. He was always brimming with ideas, and the fashion house thrived under his tenure. After losing momentum again later in the 1980s, Chloé called upon the designer in 1992 to resurrect the brand—a miracle he performed once more, and Chloé rose anew, a modern-day Lazarus. In 1997, Lagerfeld handed over the reins to Stella McCartney, a young designer who infused the brand with bold, irreverent femininity; then Phoebe Philo took over in 2001, enveloping Chloé in a sensual and sophisticated allure.

His highly graphic approach and iconic prints, his hand-painted silk crepe fabrics, his asymmetrical cuts, and the lightness of his silk and crepe de chine dresses—all combined with delicate layering—brought modernity, sensuality, and charm to a brand he redefined under the banner of a blended aesthetic. Building on

le marocain
écru.

robe et fond

le robe est
coupée à la
taille et
s'arrête à la ch

fent
au milieu
du dos.

dos et le
ntrani du de

RACHMANIN

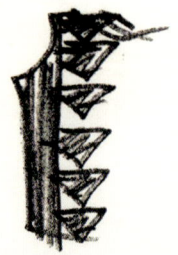

BEHIND-THE-SCENES

KARL LAGERFELD

1

2

4

2

2

4

4

4

Chloé

Renée 64

Renée

KARL LAGERFELD

Previous spread:
Lagerfeld poses
backstage with (from
left to right) Karen
Mulder, Carla Bruni,
Nadja Auermann,
Naomi Campbell,
Linda Evangelista,
Claudia Schiffer,
Helena Christensen,
and Rosemarie
Wetzel. Chloé
spring/summer 1995
ready-to-wear show,
Paris Fashion Week,
October 1994.

Left:
The "Angkor" dress,
Chloé spring/summer
1983 ready-to-
wear collection.

Right:
Olivia Wilde attends
the Met Gala in New
York on May 1, 2023,
wearing a con-
temporary version
of the Angkor dress
created by Lagerfeld
forty years earlier.

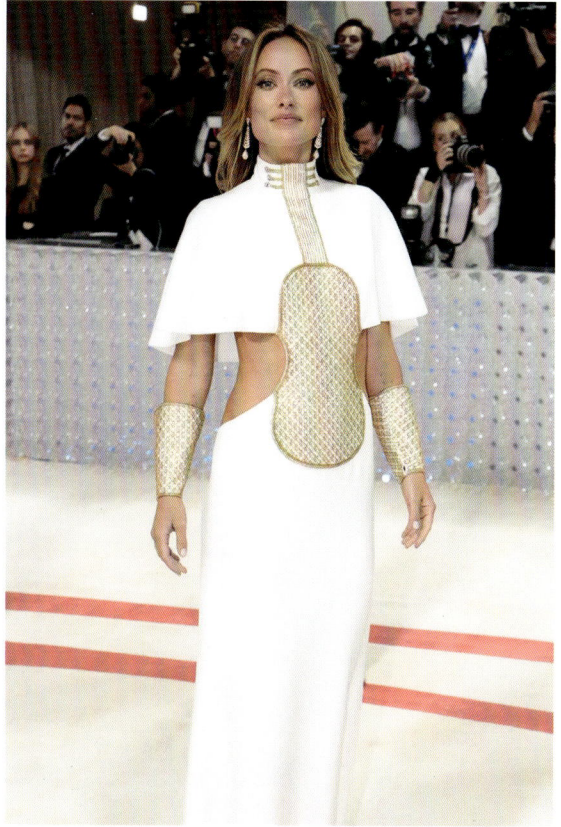

the innovative concept of luxury ready-to-wear pioneered by Aghion, Lagerfeld infused Chloé with a sense of spontaneity and celebration. On the runway, he featured young models such as Ines de la Fressange, Jerry Hall, Pat Cleveland, and Eija Vehka-Aho. At Jeannette Alfandari's Paris boutique, which sold Chloé exclusively, celebrities like Brigitte Bardot, Maria Callas, Christina Onassis, and Grace Kelly flocked to Lagerfeld's designs. In 1975, the first Chloé fragrance revolutionized the perfume world, and a decade later, Karl made a splash with his trompe l'oeil Angkor dress, often referred to as the "violin dress" for its embroidery shaped like a violin.

Lagerfeld's creative methodology was deeply influenced by Antonio Lopez, the brilliant Puerto Rican fashion illustrator and photographer, who arrived in Paris from New York in 1969 with his partner and artistic director, Juan Ramos. As journalist Alicia Drake has shown, Lopez and Ramos introduced Lagerfeld to a new approach to creation, one that infused Parisian fashion with the concept of constant renewal and tapped into the ephemeral nature of trends. Lagerfeld excelled in this fusion of eclectic inspirations, combining his vast cultural knowledge with an acute sensitivity to the spirit of his time. He soon mastered this art of synthesizing internal and external influences, succeeding in integrating street fashion, artistic

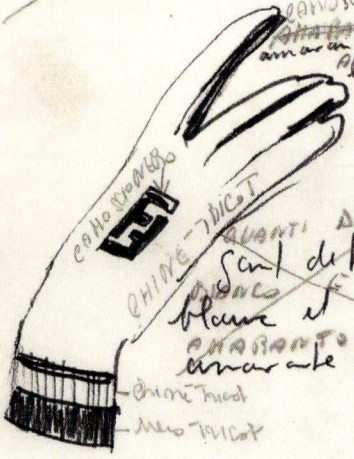

KARL LAGERFELD

Left:
Sketch by Lagerfeld
for the Fendi fall/
winter 1969-1970
collection.

Above:
Lagerfeld and the five
Fendi sisters, 1984.

Following spread, left:
Fendi fashion show,
fur collection,
fall 1984.

Right:
Fendi fall 1997
ready-to-wear show,
Milan, March 1997.

references, and personal observations into his work, in a process he described as "vampirization." "It was pick-and-mix fashion, thinking art deco today, *The Damned* tomorrow, channeling Colette last season and Fernand Léger the next. He visited every theme with huge wit, finesse, and rigor. . . . His energy was endless."[14]

While working at Chloé, Lagerfeld was approached by the Fendi family, who wanted him to transform their Rome-based brand, then specializing in furs and leather goods, into a fully-fledged, modern fashion house. The year was 1965. The contract was immediately signed between the young designer and the five Fendi sisters, and Lagerfeld immersed himself in the world of Italian fashion, then dominated by Valentino Garavani, Roberto Capucci, Emilio Pucci, and Gucci. He embraced the spirit of la dolce vita and set about revolutionizing the family business, which had been founded in 1925 by Adele and Edoardo Fendi.

His first move was the creation of a striking new logo for the house in 1965: the now-iconic double F, for "Fun Fur." His foundational gesture was to demystify fur, giving it a new lease on life by treating it like any other material and shaking up conventions. Gone were the rigid cuts, classic shapes, and heaviness. In their place came unisex collections, like the 1967 lineup featuring bomber-style fur jackets and painted furs that resembled works of art (fall/winter 1979–1980 collection). Although Lagerfeld never made provocation

KARL LAGERFELD

BEHIND-THE-SCENES

KARL LAGERFELD

a formulaic tool, he often used it to challenge norms, spark conversation, and shed light on human impulses. This was the case in 1994, when he staged a Fendi show featuring strippers and other risqué figures like adult film star Moana Pozzi. Some journalists found it scandalous and walked out of the event.

In the 1990s, the nonprofit organization PETA (People for the Ethical Treatment of Animals) launched an effort to condemn the use of animal fur. In the fashion world, the rallying cry became, "I'd rather go naked than wear fur." Growing awareness gradually led many brands to end its use, which had become synonymous with animal cruelty and scandals tied to factory farming. As consumers increasingly prioritized animal welfare, some brands began adopting innovative, non-polluting faux fur made from biomaterials, and the initiative gradually broadened, with calls for the fashion industry to eliminate all products derived from animal suffering—including leather and feathers—while seeking sustainable, low-impact alternatives.

During his longest collaboration with a fashion house (1965–2019), Lagerfeld remained committed to real fur, transforming Fendi into a luxury powerhouse. He imbued the brand with a sparkling, glamorous style—a unique blend of exuberant baroque and sobriety—that solidified its status as a symbol of Italian excellence in

KARL LAGERFELD

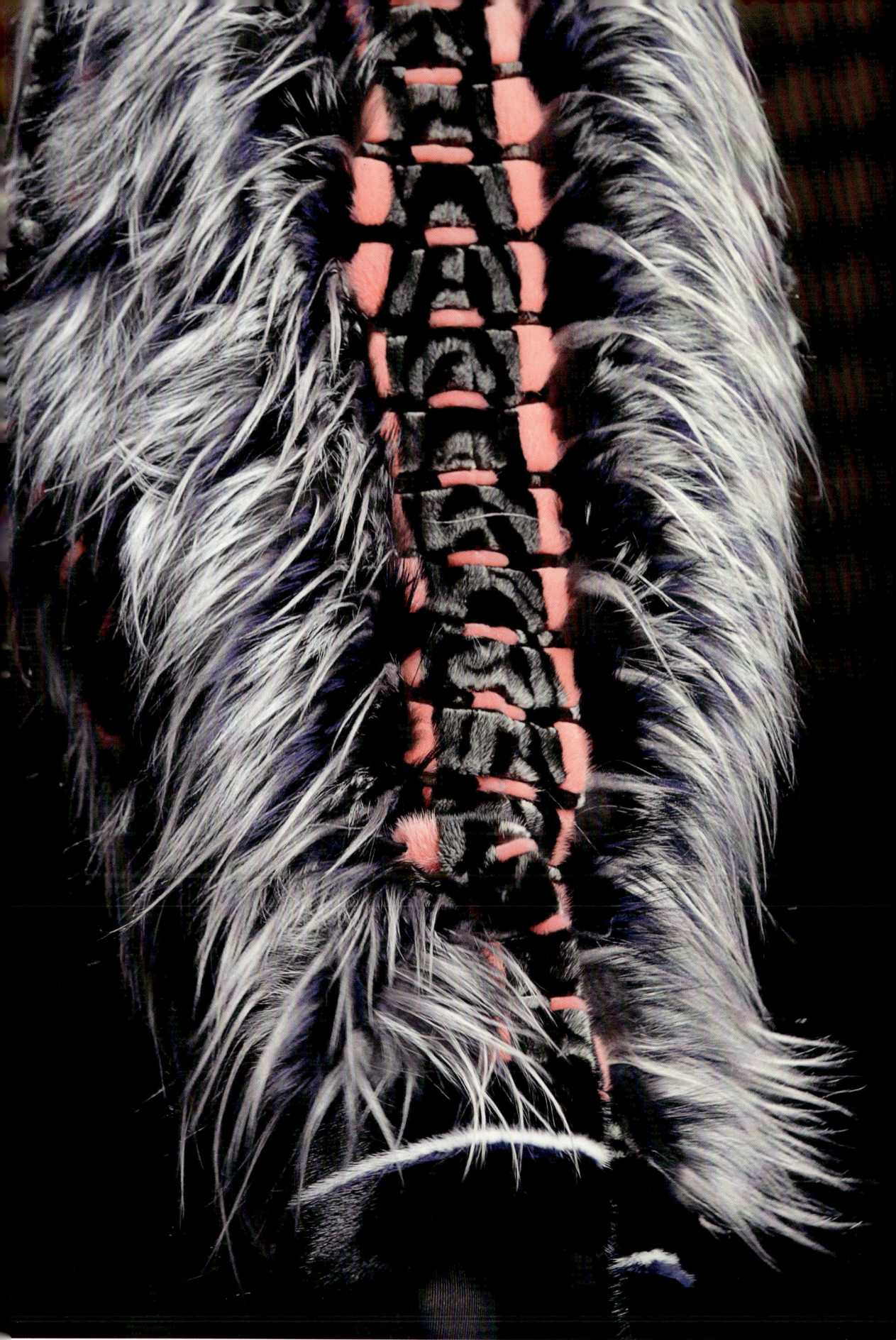

BEHIND-THE-SCENES

Below and right:
On the catwalk at
the Fendi fall/winter
2017–2018 haute
couture show for
Paris Fashion Week.

Following spread:
Fendi spring/summer
2008 fashion show
on the Great Wall of
China, October 2007.
Design by Silvia
Venturini Fendi
and Lagerfeld.

craftsmanship and savoir-faire. Under Lagerfeld's direction, the family-run business evolved into a luxury empire, expanding into men's and women's ready-to-wear, shoes, perfumes, eyewear, scarves, and sportswear in the 1970s and 1980s, before finally venturing into haute couture in 2015. Resurrection complete.

Maintaining his independence as a free-lance designer, Lagerfeld continued to juggle multiple roles, and he achieved a long-awaited but ultimate triumph in 1983, when he began his tenure as creative director at Chanel. A new chapter began as he ascended the grand art deco staircase of the eighteenth-century town house at 31 Rue Cambon, in the heart of Paris's first arrondissement.

BEHIND-THE-SCENES

119.

Left:
Lagerfeld's second
couture collection
for Chanel, with Ines
de la Fressange and
Tara Shannon.

Following spread:
Lagerfeld and Ines
de la Fressange,
fitting for the Chanel
spring/summer
1984 collection.

On January 25, 1983, the fashion world's attention was fixed on 31 Rue Cambon, where the ambitious and atypical Karl Lagerfeld was about to unveil his first Chanel show: the spring/summer 1983 haute couture collection. It would mark his long-awaited return to the world of haute couture after a two-decade hiatus. How would a man—and a German, no less—reimagine the quintessentially French elegance of Mademoiselle Chanel? It was mission impossible, according to some self-appointed guardians of tradition.

The pressure was immense, given the weight of Chanel's legacy, the economic stakes, and the challenge of revitalizing an iconic yet aging brand. And Lagerfeld was far from having full support. His appointment had sent shockwaves through the industry and devastated Yves Saint Laurent, whom Coco Chanel had seen as her spiritual heir. In the front row, luminaries such as Isabelle Adjani, Paloma Picasso, Claude Pompidou, and Marie-Hélène de Rothschild awaited the big reveal. And for the first time in Chanel's history, music backed the show, heralding the start of a new era.

The Kaiser opened the show with a tribute to France, dressing up the runway in the country's colors—though not in their traditional order. He began with a blue suit worn by Dianne deWitt, followed by a red suit modeled by Anne Rohart, and then a white suit adorned with gold chains worn by

KARL LAGERFELD

Ines de la Fressange. For months, Lagerfeld had immersed himself in the Chanel archives, acquiring an encyclopedic understanding of the house's history, the life of its founder, and the essence of Chanel's style. Driven by the challenge of balancing coherence with innovation, and fidelity to the brand's heritage with transformation, he approached the seemingly impossible task with zeal.

His debut collection paid homage to the most iconic elements of the Chanel wardrobe: the tweed-trimmed suit, the quilted chain bag, the boater hat, pearl necklaces, two-tone shoes, and black satin bows. While honoring these symbols, he reimagined them all in a spirit of metamorphosis. Skirts and suit jackets were shortened, and the timeless Chanel aesthetic was infused with fresh, contemporary images and ideas.

Reactions were mixed. Some spoke out to denounce a zest of vulgarity and an excess of accessories. The twin dilemmas of how to remain faithful without mimicking, and how much to differentiate without straying too far, were at the heart of the judgments made by the public and fashion press. In the words of *Women's Wear Daily*, "[Kaiser Karl] committed too many Chanel dont's and not enough dos." However, as author Patrick Mauriès writes,[15] this first show provided the key to Lagerfeld's subsequent shows and to his aesthetic approach. Starting with his launch collection, he began to draw on the memory of the fashion house and subtly transposed the items from its past. The references and the style constants were there, but differently.

Previous spread:
On the catwalk,
Chanel spring/
summer 2019 ready-
to-wear collection,
Paris, October 2018.

Left and above:
Chanel fall/winter
1983–1984 ready-
to-wear collection,
Paris, March 1983.

BEHIND-THE-SCENES

KARL LAGERFELD

Left:
Ines de la Fressange,
Chanel fall/winter
1989-1990 ready-
to-wear collection,
Paris, March 1989.

Below:
Chanel fall/winter
1989-1990 haute
couture show,
Paris, July 1989.

Following spread:
Frankie Rayder
and Mariacarla
Boscono on the
beach in Biarritz in an
advertising campaign
for the Chanel spring/
summer 2003 ready-
to-wear collection.

Lagerfeld's genius lay in transcending the notion of "variations on Chanel," developing a creative approach rooted in the bold fusion of Chanel's basic characteristics with the trends and aesthetics of the time. He thus managed to revitalize the brand's signature elements while ensuring the perpetuation of the iconic "CC" style. Agility was paramount, for as Lagerfeld said, "Trendy is the last stage before tacky."

The Chanel years represent the most remarkable chapter in the Lagerfeld story. From 1983 to 2019, he served as Chanel's artistic director for the brand's haute couture, ready-to-wear, and accessory lines. Hired by Alain Wertheimer, Lagerfeld often described their partnership in Faustian terms. "When I came to Chanel, I said to Mr. Wertheimer, 'Let's make a pact, like Faust with the Devil,'" Lagerfeld recounted. "But we don't know who is the Devil and who is Faust." With his first muse, de la Fressange, Lagerfeld redefined the image of women put forth by Chanel, following a simple principle. "I try to evolve Chanel's style by thinking of the line from Goethe," he said. "'Make a better future by developing elements from the past.'"

With boundless imagination, Lagerfeld reinterpreted the core elements of the brand, blending

KARL LAGERFELD

Left:
A model with
binoculars wearing a
faux-fur coat, bag, and
toque. Chanel fall/
winter 1994-1995
ready-to-wear
collection, Paris,
March 1994.

Right:
Claudia Schiffer,
Chanel spring/
summer 1994 ready-
to-wear collection,
Paris, October 1993.

Following spread, left:
Chanel spring/
summer 1987 ready-
to-wear collection,
Paris, October 1986.

Right:
Chanel spring/
summer 1994 haute
couture show, Paris
Fashion Week,
January 1993.

them with the spirit of the time and morphing them
into the "hits of the season," in the words of journalist
Marie Ottavi. He put forth a new paradigm of French
elegance, freeing it from its shackles, and redesigned
women's silhouettes. He also had a remarkable talent
for staging runway shows, and he was the pioneer of
Chanel's cruise collections. Each year, he designed
ten collections: two for haute couture, four for ready-
to-wear (two of them independent from the shows),
one cruise collection, one métiers d'art collection,
and two capsule collections (*Coco Beach* and *Coco
Neige*). The innovative way in which he reinterpreted
Chanel's codes reflected his postmodern aesthetic,
rooted in his extraordinary knowledge and memory
of the fashion landscape. He was able to play off its
echoes in the collective imagination, and he kept it
fresh by tying it in with contemporary urban trends.

In the June 1994 issue of *Vanity Fair,* Lagerfeld
described his role as Chanel's maestro: "Chanel is
composed of only a few elements," says Lagerfeld.
"White camellias, quilted bags, an Austrian door-
man's jacket, pearls, chains, shoes with black toes. I
use these elements like notes to play with. It's limited,
but I think it's great. People like it because they can
identify it—and identify *with* it. The mysterious ques-
tion is *why* they identify with it. It has something to
do with Paris, with what people know, and what
they don't know. It's not connected to any reality
anymore. Chanel has become part of the 'collective

KARL LAGERFELD

BEHIND-THE-SCENES

KARL LAGERFELD

Left:
Claudia Schiffer,
Chanel spring/
summer 1992 ready-
to-wear collection,
Paris, March 1992.

Above:
Chanel spring/
summer 2019 ready-
to-wear collection,
Paris Fashion Week,
October 2018.

unconscious.'" In another statement, he highlighted his role as both composer and performer: "I play with Chanel's elements like a musician plays with notes. You don't have to make the same music if you are a decent musician."

Lagerfeld boasted an impressive mastery of Chanel's style archives, to which he added a dose of irreverence to bring bold innovation to the brand. He revitalized its audience, appealing to youth while aiming to retain Chanel's more mature clientele. In his break with tradition, he introduced leggings in 1989 and incorporated denim into ready-to-wear collections. Lagerfeld even had models walk the runway in skintight tights, but the timing was off, and the look failed to resonate.

He introduced sneakers into haute couture and ready-to-wear at a time when it was heresy to do so. To some extent, modernizing Chanel meant challenging its heritage. Not only did he rework the classic black dress and two-tone ballet flats, drawing from rock 'n' roll and grunge influences, he appealed to the rap scene as well, and in a stroke of marketing genius, he placed the double-C logo on the label's clothing and accessories. Highly visible, the logo acted as a visual marker, providing a more defined identity and creating a community of Chanel aficionados.

The rise of logomania in fashion, where the logo becomes a visual and distinctive code for a brand, can irritate or amuse, with its ostentatious, attention-seeking nature, and it is sometimes seen as vulgar,

FLORE
MONTEX

61805

ocarabé

devant
scarabé
brode

operle
chicauses
"baguette"

scarabé

Chanel Paris NY
2018/19

KARL LAGERFELD

137.

Left:
Sketch by Lagerfeld
for the Chanel
2018-2019 *Métiers
d'Art Paris-New York*
collection, Chanel
archives, Paris.

Below:
Sketch by Lagerfeld
for the Chanel fall/
winter 2002-2003
haute couture
collection, Chanel
archives, Paris.

like leaving the price tag on for all to see. In response to this shift, and in an effort to get back closer to the real essence of fashion, designer Martin Margiela avoided any mention of his name whatsoever—he sewed blank labels into his clothes, with four white stitches exposed on the back. Ironically, given that fashion recycles everything, this anti-logo would itself become the logo of Margiela.

At Chanel, Lagerfeld applies a lyrical, Mallarméan experimentation to design. Mirroring modern poetry, he shifts fashion to free verse, with a revolution in syntax. He has the vast Chanel vocabulary at his disposal, and by inserting it into a new kind of syntax, he goes through Chanel in order to go outside of and beyond it, to hyperbolize it.

From the 1980s onward, Lagerfeld did more than simply rejuvenate Chanel; he raised it from its ashes and it took flight toward the empyrean, a phoenix reborn. While he did not sew himself, his extraordinary technical mastery and the precision of his sketches dazzled the seamstresses working under him. In the end, it is all about what to do with the gathering dust; where Hebe Dorsey, the sharp-tongued editor of the *International Herald Tribune*,

BEHIND-THE-SCENES

KARL LAGERFELD

Left:
Chanel fall/winter
1999-2000 haute
couture show,
Paris, July 1999.

Above:
Chanel fall/winter
1996-1997 ready-
to-wear collection,
Paris, March 1996.

Next page:
Linda Evangelista
photographed by
Lagerfeld. Publicity
photo for the
Chanel fall/winter
1991-1992 ready-
to-wear collection.

once declared that the dust should stay put on Chanel's shoulders, Lagerfeld swept it away with a deft, almost magical touch. Although this method of revitalizing a brand by reinterpreting its past has since become common practice in fashion, it was revolutionary in the early 1980s.

"Passing judgment on the fashion of an era is pointless. Every era has the fashion it deserves," he wrote, going on to liken fashion to the barrel of the Danaides, with a never-ending flow of new aesthetic concepts. His artistry lay in his sense of kairos—the ability to capture ideas at just the right moment—and in his talent for unveiling the underlying dynamics of the present and its hidden faces. As artist Paul Klee said, "Art does not reproduce the visible; rather, it makes visible." Lagerfeld clearly shares this view, expanding on the concept in the catalog for the 2005 Chanel exhibition at the Metropolitan Museum of Art in New York City. "Fashion is also an attempt to make certain invisible aspects of the reality of the moment visible."

At Chanel, he weathered the shifting trends over the decades, surviving the minimalist turn, and observing the fleeting mutations of the fashion scene—the rise and fall of punk, the emergence of porno chic under Tom Ford, and the ascent of the grunge, anti-fashion, and avant-garde movements (in which he never believed). He ultimately came through unscathed, though nothing was more foreign to him than the minimalist wave that swept through society in the 1990s. He managed to reinterpret the shift toward austerity, simplicity, and restraint in his

KARL LAGERFELD

"IT'S ESSENTIAL AND
NATURAL TO NOT BE LIKE
EVERYONE ELSE."

—KARL LAGERFELD

Right:
Linda Evangelista,
Chanel spring/
summer 1991 ready-
to-wear collection,
Paris Fashion Week,
October 1990.

Following spread:
Chanel 2008-2009
cruise collection,
presented at the
Raleigh Hotel in
Miami Beach on
May 15, 2008, with a
performance by the
American Olympic
synchronized
swimming team to
close the show.

own way for Chanel's wardrobe, without ceasing to embrace maximalism or betraying his own vision. He executed what he called a "visual cleansing . . . out of opportunism," while waiting for minimalism to fade from fashion.

For Lagerfeld, grace was rooted in hyperbole, not in minimalism or the mantra of "less is more." Throughout the 1990s, he observed the trends emerging from subcultures, absorbing them and remixing them with the skill of a brilliant DJ. In the process, he blurred the once-sacrosanct lines between good taste and bad, dismantling traditional cultural and normative ideas of elegance and beauty.

One of Lagerfeld's favorite techniques was a form of collage—the assembly of contrasting elements, the blending of high culture with street culture. For the spring/summer 1991 ready-to-wear collection, he sent Linda Evangelista down the runway in cycling shorts and a bright blue sequined jacket, carrying a surfboard. Likewise, under Lagerfeld, hip-hop fashion emerged from the Bronx to walk the runway: the caps, thick gold chains, and over-size rap-style belts of the milieu were repurposed, reimagined, and recycled by Chanel. This pursuit of visual tension between discordant elements deeply unsettled Yves Saint Laurent, who viewed it as a betrayal of Chanel's essence. "Today, this profession is in decline," he remarked. "I can't understand it. At Chanel, they have chains everywhere, strips of

BEHIND-THE-SCENES

Left:
A model at the
Chanel supermarket,
fall/winter 2014-
2015 ready-to-wear
collection, Paris
Fashion Week,
March 2014.

Right:
Carmen Kass, Chanel
spring/summer
2011 ready-to-wear
collection, Paris,
October 2010.

Following spread:
Arctic landscape at
the Chanel fall/winter
2010-2011 ready-
to-wear collection,
Paris, March 2010.

leather. The poor woman must be rolling over in her grave."[16] Perhaps—but this was precisely the effect Lagerfeld intended to achieve.

To say that Lagerfeld revitalized Chanel would be an understatement. For more than three decades, under his leadership and in collaboration with Virginie Viard (who succeeded him as artistic director of Chanel's fashion collections after his passing), the brand achieved unprecedented global renown. Sales soared, and the number of stores worldwide multiplied. Lagerfeld's constant reimagination and renewal served a creative vision characterized by coherence and humor, while his spectacular and magical shows—an element he had pioneered at Chloé in the 1970s—became some of the most eagerly anticipated events in fashion. One striking example is the fall/winter 2010-2011 ready-to-wear show where, perhaps to raise awareness of global warming, he had artists sculpt blocks of ice into iceberg shapes. At the Grand Palais, his grandiose shows featured elaborate, eclectic, and at times pharaonic decors: a supermarket, a giant golden lion, a replica of the Eiffel Tower, even an airport. Meanwhile, the métiers d'art collections paid tribute to the craftsmanship and excellence of Chanel's ateliers, as well as those of Lesage and Montex (embroidery), Lemarié (feathers and artificial flowers), Causse (gloves), Massaro

KARL LAGERFELD

BEHIND-THE-SCENES

KARL LAGERFELD

BEHIND-THE-SCENES

KARL LAGERFELD

Previous spread:
Chanel spring/
summer 2011 haute
couture show, Paris,
January 2011.

Left:
Lagerfeld and the
models on the beach
runway, Chanel
spring/summer
2019 ready-to-wear
collection, Paris,
October 2018.

(shoes), Goossens (jewelry making), Michel (milli-nery), and Lognon (pleating).

The 1980s also saw the birth of the Karl Lagerfeld brand, created by a man who had, for decades, refused to establish his own label. In 1984, he launched his namesake fashion house while continuing to design countless collections each year for Chanel, Fendi, and others. However, his personal line, KL, never achieved significant success and finally went bankrupt in 1997, as Lagerfeld gradually lost interest over the years. True to form, though, Lagerfeld resus-citated the brand the following year—yet another phoenix in his aviary—as Lagerfeld Gallery, before it returned to the name Karl Lagerfeld in 2012.

In 2004, he collaborated with H&M on a collection of thirty pieces. It was a triumph. "He's like a living library," said Donald Schneider, the artistic director for H&M who worked with Lagerfeld on the advertising campaign. "He uses cultural history as an instrument, but then he reshapes it in a modern context. And we are not talking just simple refer-ences from fashion magazines; he goes way back in history. He knows what color Catherine the Great liked for her bedroom."[17] For Lagerfeld, fashion corresponded to the definition given by Victoire de Castellane, who worked alongside him at Chanel as a jewelry designer before later moving on to Dior: "Fashion is an antidepressant. And fashion is our French Hollywood."[18]

AESTHETIC

Aesthetic

KARL LAGERFELD

"I am a black diamond, unfaceted. Black diamonds are rare, hard to cut, and therefore uncommercial."

—Karl Lagerfeld

LAGERFELD'S VOCABULARY

What is Karl Lagerfeld's signature style, if any, given his versatility and numerous collaborations? Is there a common thread, some kind of foundational aesthetic vocabulary running through his collections? Can we identify any stylistic tendencies, or a preference for certain shapes, materials, or colors? When fashion historians and designers compare the work of the two couturiers who most influenced twentieth-century fashion—Yves Saint Laurent and Lagerfeld—they typically contrast the purity of the former with the postmodernity of the latter. Stylist Gilles Dufour, who collaborated with Lagerfeld at Chanel and Fendi, expands on this perspective. "Karl had no limits, no inhibitions," he says. "These weren't pure creations like those of Yves Saint Laurent, but Karl was a true stylist with an ultra-intelligent sense of fashion. With him, things moved forward. He absorbed everything."[19]

Lagerfeld positioned his creations as the antithesis of the Saint Laurent aesthetic. Fashion historian Florence Müller identifies a common thread running through Lagerfeld's work. "The 1920s and 1930s are very significant. He had a fascination with the interwar period, which he adapted for Chanel and especially Chloé, with the use of crepe de chine, highly fluid materials, pleated and flowing skirts, small tops like those worn on beaches in the 1930s, pastel tones, soft greens and blues, shades of ivory. . . ."[20] Behind the mask, certain constants thus start to emerge: a predilection for fluidity and soft lines, an affinity for black and white, and a deep connection to the fashion of the 1930s.

Lagerfeld's creative DNA is defined by freshness, modernity, and audacity—it is more a matter of *Stimmungen*, or "atmospheres," than any singular, recognizable signature. He shaped fashion by focusing on the overall look, his vision of elegance, and a connection to the zeitgeist over the creation of distinct, identifiable lines. In *The Allure of Chanel*, based on his conversations with Coco Chanel, Paul Morand writes, "Where then does the couturier's genius lie? The genius is in anticipating . . . Fashion is a matter of speed . . . I often hear it said that ready-made clothes are killing fashion. Fashion wants to be killed; it is designed for that."[21] Lagerfeld's aesthetic vocabulary reflects that of a man of letters, a polyglot,

1969   1978   1983

1992   1994   1997

2003   2007   2009

2017   2017   2018

KARL LAGERFELD

and an insatiable aesthete. In the world of fashion, he brought to life Baudelaire's famous verse from *The Flowers of Evil*: "You gave me your mud, and I have turned it into gold."

For an example of Lagerfeld's transmutational powers, let us consider one of Chanel's timeless classics: the 2.55 handbag, named for its creation in February 1955. Featuring a chain shoulder strap and quilted lambskin, the bag has become a cult object. And during Lagerfeld's time at Chanel, he built on the original design to breathe new life into this iconic piece, reimagining it through countless iterations, as well as proposing new offerings (like the Chanel Boy bag, which blends masculine and feminine energy). Using the bag's basic elements—quilted patterns, the metallic chain, and the double-C logo—he composed a visual symphony, exploring harmonies between shapes and materials and contrasts between rigidity and fluidity, as well as between colors. His experimentation led to a series of unforgettable and surprising designs crafted in tweed, denim, or with sequins, as Lagerfeld expanded the bag's legacy. The 11.12 offers a similar story. While it made its debut in the 1970s, it was Lagerfeld's reinterpretation in the 1980s that elevated it to new heights of desirability, establishing an intimate dialogue with the timeless beauty of the 2.55. For Lagerfeld, designing an accessory meant reimagining it entirely.

In a Platonic vein, one might say that all thought relies on reminiscence. Among the most iconic models and variations imagined by the designer are the Chanel Girl, the Chanel 31, and the Chanel 19. During the Chanel spring/summer 2019 ready-to-wear show, the Chanel bag was transformed into a seashell, while for the Chanel cruise 2019 show, Lagerfeld surprised audiences with a clutch shaped like a life preserver. In these stylistic exercises—all variations on themes composed by Chanel—the most improbable forms take center

Left:
Handbag, Chanel fall/
winter 2017–2018
ready-to-wear
collection, Paris.

Right:
Handbag, Chanel
spring/summer
2018 ready-to-wear
collection, Paris.

Following spread:
Lagerfeld
photographed by
Helmut Newton
in 1983 at 31 Rue
Cambon in Paris.

stage, such as at the Chanel spring/summer 2018 ready-to-wear show, where Lagerfeld's disco ball clutch dazzled the audience. These constant reinventions pay homage to the building blocks of the bags originally imagined by Chanel while transforming them into unusual, extravagant, and ultradesirable objects—sometimes provocative, and always marked by elegance, whimsy, and humor. The breadth of the models conceived by Lagerfeld is truly remarkable, including designs like a rocket clutch, a small plexiglass clutch in the shape of a Chanel No. 5 perfume bottle, a robot, a spool of golden thread, a powder compact, an LED bag, a golden gas can, a banana, a camera, a mushroom, a Hula-Hoop, a plate, a LEGO brick, a milk carton, a supermarket basket, a plexiglass tote, and even a shipping container.

Behind the language of fashion lies an empire of impulses and the power they exert—whereby fashion becomes like a drug, fostering an almost narcotic dependency, and gives rise to a kind of mystical fervor.

KARL LAGERFELD

AESTHETIC

MADEMOIS
PRIVÉ

KARL LAGERFELD

AESTHETIC

KARL LAGERFELD

POSTMODERNISM

Karl Lagerfeld's vision of fashion, his philosophy of aesthetics, and the realization of his ideas align with the paradigm of postmodernism. Without delving into the controversies surrounding this epistemological and aesthetic concept, which encompasses heterogeneous realities, it can be asserted that the postmodernism of his creations lies in a set of distinctive characteristics. This includes blending references to the past and fashion heritage with contemporary elements; fusing popular and high culture (implying the rejection of traditional hierarchies); recycling existing designs and concepts; the art of collage, particularly with regard to his sources of inspiration; and the practice of repurposing. In literature, architecture, music, design, and fashion, postmodernism is less a historical period than a worldview shared by a range of creators.

To Yves Saint Laurent's pure compositions, Lagerfeld counters with his fireworks—a mastery of mixing that is grounded in a unique ability to reflect and anticipate the unconscious zones of the zeitgeist. If Lagerfeld succeeded in reinventing Chanel, it is because he dismissed the orthodoxy and idolatry that stifle the creative spirit with their weight of deference. He absorbed the atmosphere, the soul of the fashion house, before injecting his own aesthetic—and, most importantly, that of the present. His postmodernism was rooted in his extraordinary memory and encyclopedic knowledge of fashion history. Drawing from this vast reservoir of forms, memories, and notes, he transformed the constraints of heritage into radically innovative aesthetic proposals— notably through collage. What might seem at first like frivolous child's play was in fact a way to tap into his unfailing sense of composition and his genius for sparking consumer desire. He sacralized the profane, profaned the sacred, played with contrasts, blended the trivial and the austere, broke with tradition through the use of offbeat elements, and introduced original concepts on which he built entire collections. This approach is exemplified by the Chanel spring/summer 2007 haute couture collection, created around the concept of "vertical flexibility."

The fashion world—with its history, trends, and evolution—was to Lagerfeld like an immense library, every shelf of which he knew intimately. It was a Tower of Babel to which he made his

Lagerfeld in front
of the shelves at
his Paris bookshop,
the Librairie 7L.

own additions—in silk, velvet, cotton, and wool. An accomplished polyglot, Lagerfeld's passion extended to actual books as well, as evidenced by his 2011 perfume called Paper Passion, an olfactory creation with notes evoking the scent of paper. It was this same love of literature that inspired him to open his bookstore in 1999, located at 7 Rue de Lille in Paris's seventh arrondissement, followed by his publishing house, 7L, in 2001, which specialized in photography and poetry books.

If his immense artistic culture nourished his creations, it was never through a process of immediate export-import or direct transfusion. The copy-paste method, where a source of inspiration is catapulted wholesale into a collection, was not his style. A devoted admirer of writer Jorge Luis Borges, Lagerfeld shared with him a fascination for labyrinths and aesthetic meta-construction. His postmodernism was unique in its ability to combine aristocratic elitism with creations designed for the many. In one of his interviews with *Vogue Paris*, he spoke of his love for cinema, citing some of the films that had marked him the most. While it may not be possible to pinpoint any single collection or item that stemmed directly from these, their influence subtly permeated his collections. As he told *Vogue*, dashing through his personal hit parade: "*Children of Paradise* was the first French film I saw in Hamburg. I fell under the spell of María Casares's character in *The Ladies of the Bois de Boulogne* because she shares my taste for petty revenge. I love the graphic style of *The Cabinet of Dr. Caligari*, and I think *The Others* is one of the best contemporary films and undoubtedly Nicole Kidman's finest role. There's also *L'Inhumaine* by Marcel L'Herbier, for which I have a watercolor presentation model. Aside from that, I am a specialist in German silent films. Every image is an image, and I like that. Take for example *Metropolis* by Fritz Lang, Brigitte Helm's first film, which remains modern even today. And, without wanting to sound snobbish, I'm fascinated by Swedish cinema from the 1920s, particularly *The Saga of Gösta Berling*, directed by Mauritz Stiller. The funeral procession on the lake is an absolutely magical scene."[22]

AESTHETIC

KARL LAGERFELD

Jacqueline de Ribes
and Lagerfeld at Le
Palace in Paris.

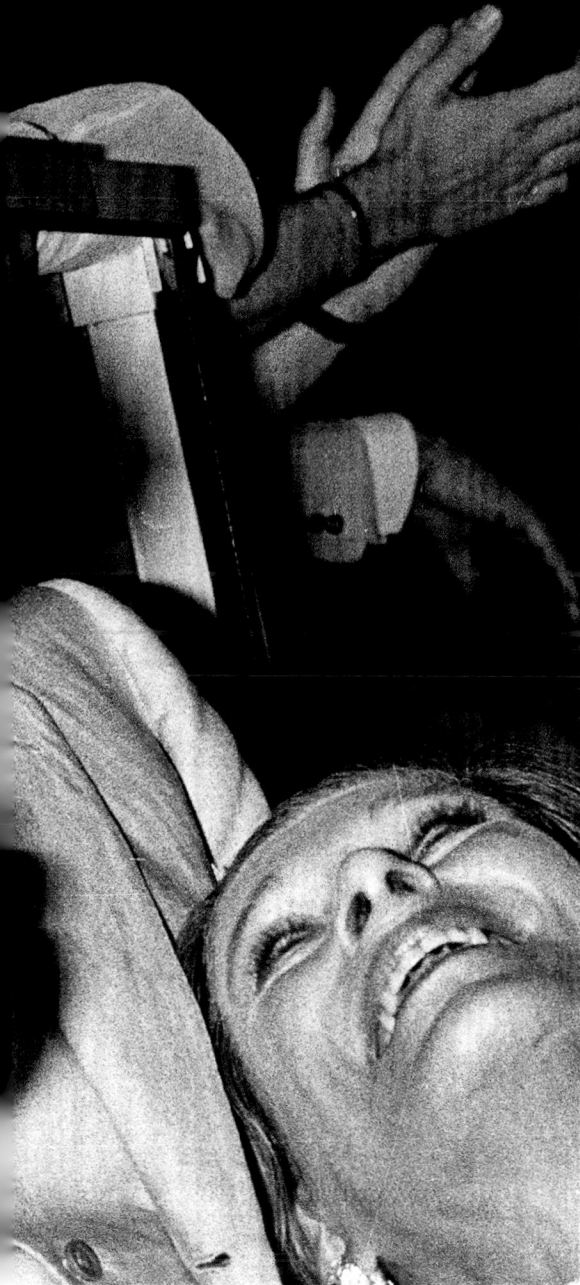

Much like his bestselling life story, Karl Lagerfeld's designs reshaped the codes of fashion in the era of globalization. He was a true icon, but one of conscious and careful construction, begetting his characteristic—even fetishistic—look: a white shirt with a high, starched collar, a tie adorned with a jewel, a black jacket, dark sunglasses, black leather gloves, ostentatious rings, and a low ponytail. In this way, Lagerfeld, a self-styled "mercenary" of fashion, shielded himself behind the fiction of his own legend, aided by his sharp wit, rapid-fire delivery, and bold outspokenness (which often clashed with political correctness). Always just out of reach, he played on fashion's core dialectic of being versus seeming in order to present a public-facing image that revealed nothing of his deeper, esoteric self.

His deliberate media overexposure, carried off with flair and a sharp sense of marketing, allowed him to further conceal his true self. And this cultivation of mystery extended to his creations as well. He blurred lines everywhere, refusing to be confined by any kind of label or formula. As journalist Marie Ottavi observed, while Lagerfeld did display certain tendencies, "[f]or Karl, to leave an imprint too deeply, and to cling to it, is to run the risk of one day becoming obsolete. As one anonymous observer notes, 'It is difficult to attribute to him a specific silhouette, certain proportions, a look, or a way of carrying oneself. Style is obsessive, ritualistic, repetitive, and recognizable at first glance—and Karl hated that.'"[23]

KARL LAGERFELD

Left:
Transparent dress
embroidered with
glittering cameras,
Chloé spring/summer
1974 collection.

Below:
Fendi fall/winter
2016–2017 show,
Milan Fashion Week,
February 2016.

SIGNATURE CREATIONS

Karl Lagerfeld's extraordinary legacy includes historic designs, iconic masterpieces, and spectacular fashion shows that still resonate today. The selection below offers a closer look at a few unforgettable creations that have left a lasting mark on fashion history, chosen subjectively and presented in no particular order. Of course, countless other standout moments from the Kaiser could have been included as well—a testament to the boundless creativity and lasting influence of his work in the fashion world.

The Angkor dress introduced in the Chloé spring/summer 1983 collection stands out as one of his most notable designs. It encapsulates the essence of the 1980s, exuding the unmistakable spirit of the era with its golden, instrument-like design. This dress embodies the Chloé attitude—a blend of freshness, humor, and elegance. Built on a trompe l'œil concept, it plays with contrasts and ambiguity. Viewed from the back, it resembles a bolero paired with a straight skirt, but its true nature is revealed only from the front. Hugging the body's curves with a bold sensuality, the dress features violin-like cutouts reminiscent of Man Ray's famous photograph *Le Violon d'Ingres*, where the nude back of Kiki de Montparnasse is adorned with a violin's f-holes. The surrealist spirit of Man Ray is seamlessly translated into Lagerfeld's so-called violin dress. This black-and-gold ensemble, enhanced with rhinestones, pearls, and a jeweled officer collar, strikes a balance between aristocratic refinement and playful mischief. After Roger Vadim's *And God Created Woman*, Lagerfeld creates the violin-woman.

Another standout Chloé design is the transparent black dress from the spring/summer 1974 collection, worn by Sylvie Vartan in *Vogue Paris* that same year. This piece combines an organza skirt with a slip dress, adorned with silver sequins and glass tube beads, creating a shimmering symphony of textures. As for Fendi, for the fall/winter 2016–2017 Haute Fourrure show, Lagerfeld unveiled an unprecedented piece: a coat composed of countless tiny squares of mink, requiring 1,200 hours of meticulous assembly.

The designer's boundless imagination and overflowing creativity reached new heights during the decades he spent elevating Chanel. Let us indulge in the inherently subjective exercise of highlighting a few emblematic looks that helped shape the multifaceted image of the Lagerfeldian woman—a notion marked by profusion but at the same time singular, infused with the unique spiritual energy the designer brought to his creations. Brushing aside chronology, we turn will turn first to the elegant black dress adorned with gold chains from the Chanel spring/summer 1992 haute couture collection. This masterpiece, now part of fashion history, was first worn on the runway by Christy Turlington, then donned by Penélope Cruz in Pedro Almodóvar's 2009 film *Broken Embraces*, before turning up again a decade later at the 2019 Met Gala, worn by Lily-Rose Depp.

Countless breathtaking wedding dresses stand out among Lagerfeld's creations. One could first cite the slender white dress under a feathered cape worn by model Alek Wek in 2004, or the floral dress and veil worn by Claudia Schiffer at the spring/summer 1993 haute couture show. Other unforgettable designs that might tempt someone to marry and remarry just to wear them include: the cybernuptial dress from the fall/winter 1985–1986 haute couture show; the ethereal, feather-adorned dress worn by Natalia Vodianova at the spring/summer 2003 haute couture show; the futuristic pearly white suit and elaborate paper headdress from the spring/summer 2009 haute couture show; the pastel gown with a fitted coat featuring embroidery reminiscent of the ceremonial uniforms of the so-called "Immortals" of the Académie Française (the utmost authority on the French language), shown during the fall/winter 2018–2019 haute couture show; the sleeveless jacket paired with high-waisted pants, thin-heeled boots, and a feather cape and train, blending feminine and masculine codes, presented at the spring/summer 2018 haute couture show; and finally, Lagerfeld's last bridal creation: a silver one-piece swimsuit with a dramatic train, worn by Vittoria Ceretti at the spring/summer 2019 haute couture show. Through his wedding dresses, Lagerfeld conveyed his vision of the era and shifts in society, as when he presented two brides at the spring/summer 2013 haute couture show to take a stand in support of same-sex marriage and marriage equality in France.[24]

On numerous occasions, Lagerfeld unveiled dresses fit for a fairy-tale princess, like the breathtaking dress from the fall/winter 1991–1992 haute couture collection worn by Christy Turlington, featuring a layered skirt in lilac organza, embellished with jewels. To complete the look, Turlington wore a shawl, oversize earrings,

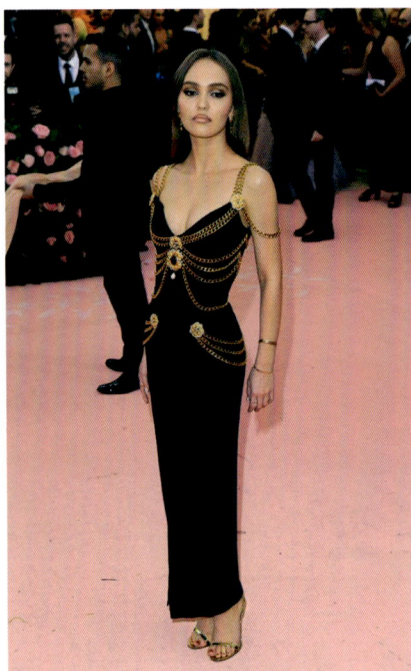

AESTHETIC

KARL LAGERFELD

AESTHETIC

KARL LAGERFELD

Left:
Supermodel Helena
Christensen with
a blazer and denim
skirt over a fishnet
bodysuit, Chanel fall/
winter 1991–1992
ready-to-wear
collection, Paris.

Below:
Naomi Campbell,
Chanel spring/
summer 1994
show, Paris.

Following spread:
Lagerfeld backstage at
the Chloé fall/winter
1976 show, which
featured Coromandel-
inspired motifs.

Pages 186-7:
Chanel fall/winter
2013-2014 ready-
to-wear collection,
Paris Fashion Week,
March 2013.

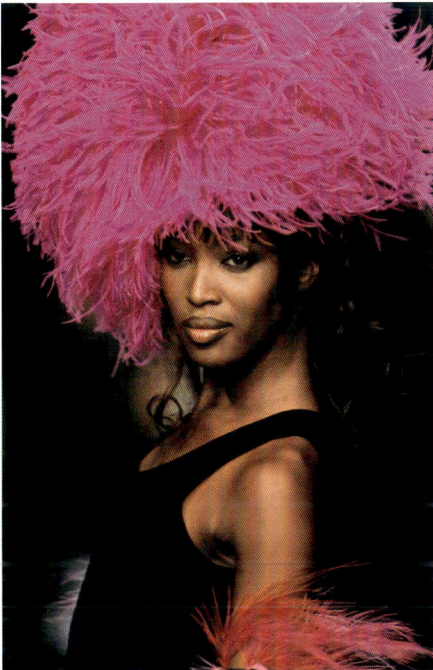

and crystal bracelets, delivering a burst of story-book magic. The spring/summer 1994 haute couture collection is often hailed as a stylistic pinnacle for Lagerfeld—or at the very least one of his standout moments—given its radiant energy and boldness. Among its iconic pieces was the show-stopping look worn by Naomi Campbell: a daringly short black dress paired with an oversize pink marabou hat and sheer gloves. Meanwhile, the fall/winter 1991–1992 ready-to-wear collection radiated provocation and unapologetic sass, featuring T-shirts dripping with gold chains and pearls—taking inspiration from the rap scene and Madonna—alongside frayed skirts, leather caps, and denim ensembles.

Blending medieval fashion, gothic armor, and a futuristic edge, the fall/winter 2013–2014 ready-to-wear collection takes the Chanel brand in a new direction, with striking designs: tunics, dark quilted jackets adorned with breastplates, thigh-high boots embellished with chains, and studded gloves. Coco Chanel's deep admiration for Coromandel screens embodies one of the brand's defining elements. Named after a coastal region in India, these lacquered screens, covered with intricate patterns, originate from Chinese art and reached their peak in the eighteenth century. A devoted collector—she reportedly had about twenty of them at the fashion house's headquarters—Chanel often drew inspiration from their motifs for jewelry and haute couture. In her 1958 haute couture collection, she presented a suit with a lamé lining that echoed Coromandel patterns. Lagerfeld continued this homage in his fall/winter 1996–1997 haute couture collection, featuring long coats and jackets embroidered with Coromandel-inspired designs that created what he called a "stiletto body"—a long and lean silhouette. Reinterpreting Chanel's golden dresses and reviving the founding spirit of the brand, one long evening gown featured Lesage embroidery that required hundreds of hours of needlework. This historic piece borders on perfection. Even as early as 1976, with Chloé, Lagerfeld had begun to use Coromandel motifs in his designs.

Never lacking vivid imagery to describe his collections, he referred to an "over-refinement on the border of hysteria" when characterizing the standout pieces from the spring/summer 1997 haute couture collection, from lightweight suits to high jewelry creations that embody the very essence of hyper-luxury and the spirit of Chanel. "It's [about] pushing the Chanel proportions to the edge," he said.

KARL LAGERFELD

AESTHETIC

INFLUENCE

Influence

Lagerfeld, Natalie
Portman, and
Benjamin Millepied
at the opening of
the exhibition *Esprit
Dior, Miss Dior,*
Galerie Courbe,
Grand Palais, Paris,
November 12, 2013.

Rather than the term "jack-of-all-trades," which is
both vague and inadequate—implying, as it does,
a certain dilettantism—I would instead frame
Karl Lagerfeld as an aesthete. Under Lagerfeld's
particular brand of aesthetics, his life's work can
be seen as both a defense and an illustration of the
concept of the *Gesamtkunstwerk*, or total work of
art, a notion born in the nineteenth century from
German Romanticism. Lagerfeld had the keenest
eye for detail, and he immersed himself in each
stage of the creative process, designing and
overseeing everything from beginning to end—
from the initial sketches to the runway shows and
advertising campaigns. This comprehensive vision
was made possible by his extraordinary range of
expertise across multiple artistic fields. While
primarily a fashion designer, the Kaiser was also a
skilled artist, perfumer, photographer, filmmaker,
interior designer, and publisher.

Dedicated to the ideal of the total work
of art, he approached fashion as a crystallization
of diverse artistic disciplines, interconnected yet
independent, coming together to celebrate the
union of art and life—a celebration evocative of
dandyism. The concept of the *Gesamtkunstwerk*
was first proposed by the painter and writer Philipp
Otto Runge (1777–1810), then further developed
and brought to prominence by composer Richard
Wagner (1813–1883). A century later, Lagerfeld,

KARL LAGERFELD

Left:
Stéphane Audran,
Lagerfeld, and Jane
Seymour, July 1984.

Below:
The Twist by
Claude Chabrol,
with Jean-Pierre
Cassel and Stéphane
Audran, 1976.

the ultimate multifaceted creator, achieved his own synthesis of the arts, establishing a vision of aesthetics as the convergence of many disparate mediums.

Alongside his work in fashion, Lagerfeld created dance, opera, and movie costumes. A noted music lover, he designed stage costumes for the Paris Opera (with choreographer Benjamin Millepied, for George Balanchine's *Brahms-Schoenberg Quartet* in 2016), La Scala in Milan (Hector Berlioz's *Les Troyens* in 1982), the Florence Opera (Jacques Offenbach's *The Tales of Hoffmann* in 1980), and the Opéra de Monte-Carlo (Vincenzo Bellini's *Norma* in 2009, and with choreographer Jean-Christophe Maillot for *Altro Canto* in 2006). For the silver screen, he designed costumes for many productions, including *Babette's Feast* by Gabriel Axel, and several movies by Claude Chabrol, including *Dr. Popaul*, *The Twist*, *Wedding in Blood*, and *Violette*, where he provided the wardrobe for Stéphane Audran. Forming an artistic collaboration with Audran, Lagerfeld continued to work with her over the years, designing costumes for such movies as Luis Buñuel's *The Discreet Charm of the Bourgeoisie*, Bertrand Tavernier's *Clean Slate*, and Guy Green's *The Devil's Advocate*. He also collaborated on *Mistress* by Barbet Schroeder (creating the costumes for Bulle Ogier as the dominatrix Ariane); the short film *Life Without Zoe* (Francis Ford Coppola) from the anthology film *New York Stories*; *High Heels* and *Broken Embraces* by Pedro Almodóvar; and *Callas Forever* by Franco Zeffirelli.

It was the end of the 1980s when Lagerfeld took up photography. Never one to go lightly, he delved into portraits, fashion photography, nudes, and landscapes, exploring his subjects' form, light, framing, and emotion, his work unified by the singularity of his gaze. A great admirer of black-and-white, and a collector of works by Helmut Newton, Alfred Stieglitz, André Kertész, Paul Strand, Edward Steichen, Peter Lindbergh, Steven Meisel, Bruce Weber, and many others, he delivered a sophisticated inner world, offering a plurality of motifs and techniques. "People always want to know from me what my photographic style is. I can't say," he explained. "Those who look at my pictures should say. I don't have any style, but

KARL LAGERFELD

many or none. You must not stand still, not in life, not in fashion, and not in photography."[25]

For his photography books, Lagerfeld had a long-running collaboration with German publisher Steidl. These volumes explore the echoes and parallels between the architecture of the human body and that of landscapes and cities, while also delving into the worlds of fashion and celebrity portraits. Though he had a predilection for black-and-white, he also hand-painted some of his photographs. In an interview with author Andrew Wilkes, he reflected on his approach to photography and fashion: "Everything gives me inspiration. I think Madonna is divine. I think she is it. I'm not sure I'm the right photographer for her, but I think she's great. All of these areas of popular culture helped to make up the 1980s. I don't believe in closed eyes. I am like an antenna on a building—I receive all those images."[26] Once more, there were Lagerfeld's famous animallike antennae, that overdeveloped radar system that allowed him to tune into the mindset of an era. His multisensory instincts even find a curious echo in nature, as seen in the Australian jumping spider named *Jotus karllagerfeldi* by scientists. This spider, with its black-and-white patterns reminiscent of Lagerfeld's signature style—white shirt, black gloves, and sunglasses—bears a tribute to his unmistakable aesthetic.

Lagerfeld's immense legacy, including his lasting influence on contemporary fashion, is built on the foundation of a richly complex creative universe and a vision that transcended boundaries, crossing multiple disciplines. Lagerfeld viewed the world through his own multifaceted lens, helping him to see fashion in a new and unconventional way.

LEGACY

Left page:
Lagerfeld and Virginie
Viard overlooking the
Chanel 2018-2019
cruise collection
fashion show,
Paris, May 2018.

Following spread, left:
Publicity photo for the
Chanel fall/winter
1996-1997 ready-
to-wear collection,
with Stella Tennant.

Right:
Stella Tennant
photographed by
Lagerfeld. Press
kit photo for the
Chanel fall/winter
1997-1998 haute
couture collection.

Karl Lagerfeld's influence, impact, and legacy in the fashion world are vast, standing in stark contrast to his seeming desire to fade into the background. He is among the rare designers who left an indelible mark on the fashion universe and collective imagination of his time, becoming both an icon and a legendary figure. As the kaiser of fashion, a self-styled mercenary, and a global star, his cultural footprint was large and ever growing. He featured in films and countless documentaries, and he even inspired characters in animated films and novels. With his spirited sketches and unique vision, he disrupted and redefined the codes of Chanel, Fendi, and Chloé, ensuring the fashion world avoided stagnation from the inertia of repetition or—just as noxious—the chaotic burst of gratuitous, directionless innovations. Beyond being a designer, he became what many regarded as the ultimate icon—even if no era's icons are truly definitive, as there are always others waiting in the wings.

Lagerfeld lived on the cutting edge, always looking toward the future. But he didn't turn his back on the present—he was instead captivated by the idea of an eternal present, constantly renewed and ever-turning. Summing up his philosophy of life with the kind of provocative wit he was known for, he once said, "I throw everything away. The most important piece of furniture in a house is the

KARL LAGERFELD

INFLUENCE

KARL LAGERFELD

garbage can!"[27] This erudite scholar and man of culture, who consistently drew from treasures both past and present, left behind a vision of fashion and a perspective on visual representation that were entirely personal yet unmistakably contemporary. Unshaken by the passage of time, he navigated the shifting eras and styles with aplomb, playing a pivotal role in transforming fashion. During the explosive sixties, marked by Swinging London, the hippie movement, and the liberation of society's morals, Lagerfeld was at Chloé, elevating bohemian chic to new heights. Moving into the 1970s, an era defined by fluidity, creativity, and the influences of punk, glam rock, and disco, Lagerfeld then doubled down on his independent and maverick spirit to navigate through.

From the 1980s onward, with his arrival at Chanel, Lagerfeld reigned over the runways for four decades, confronting the materialistic shift in fashion as it became a symbol of consumerism. The 1980s marked an era of hedonism, celebration, and the cult of the body. It was the Le Palace generation. Paris once again became the beating heart of fashion, fueled by the bold creativity of Jean Paul Gaultier, Thierry Mugler, Claude Montana, Azzedine Alaïa, and the rise of Japanese designers such as Rei Kawakubo, with her anti-fashion manifesto, and Yohji Yamamoto. Lagerfeld's incredible longevity, such a rare feat in the fashion industry, is mirrored by his enduring influence. For over sixty years, he reshaped the fashion world with creations that were seared into onlookers' retinas, electrifying our senses and slicing through the currents of time. Uninterested in the idea of grooming successors, he instead devoted himself to reshaping our ideals of beauty with sharp intuition.

NOTES

1. *Kaiser Karl*, Raphaëlle Bacqué, Éditions Albin Michel, Paris 2019, pp. 82 and 164.

2. *The Beautiful Fall: Fashion, Genius, and Glorious Excess in 1970s Paris*, Alicia Drake, Bloomsbury Publishing, London, 2012, p. 377.

3. Ibid., p. 236.

4. *Le monde selon Karl*, Jean-Christophe Napias and Patrick Mauriès, Flammarion, Paris 2013.

5. "Les livres préférés de Karl Lagerfeld," *Vogue Paris*, September 10, 2017.

6. *Karl: Une histoire de la mode*, Marie Ottavi, Robert Laffont, Arion Collection, Paris, 2023, p. 566.

7. *Le Corps glorieux de la top-modèle*, Véronique Bergen, Éditions Lignes, Fécamp (France), 2013.

8. See: *Jacques de Bascher: Dandy de l'ombre*, Marie Ottavi, Séguier, Paris, 2017. New edition by Plon, 2021.

9. *Sans départir*, Diane de Beauvau-Craon, Grasset, Paris, 2022.

10. "To fill a Gap" (546*), Emily Dickinson*, Emily Dickinson, Barnes & Noble Books, New York, p. 51.

11. *Anna Chronique: Un diario di moda*, Anna Piaggi and Karl Lagerfeld, Longanesi, Italy, 1986.

12. *Anna Piaggi, une visionnaire de la mode*, directed by Alina Marazzi, 2016. Cited in *Karl: Une histoire de la mode*, p. 245.

13. *Chanel défilés: L'intégrale de ses collections (depuis 1983)*, Adélia Sabatini, introduction by Patrick Mauriès, La Martinière, Paris, 2020, p. 14.

14. *The Beautiful Fall*, op. cit., p. 129.

15. *Chanel défilés: L'intégrale de ses collections*, op. cit., p. 13.

16. *Le monde selon Karl*, op. cit., p. 146.

17. *The Beautiful Fall*, op. cit., p. 153.

18. "Victoire de Castellane, la créatrice de joaillerie Dior," Loïc Prigent, *Vanity Fair*, October 28, 2014.

19. *Karl: Une histoire de la mode*, op. cit., p. 336.

20. Ibid., p. 435.

21. *The Allure of Chanel*, Paul Morand, translated by Euan Cameron, Pushkin Press, 2013, pp. 172–176.

22. "Souvenirs, secrets de style, inspirations . . . L'interview mode de Karl Lagerfeld pour *Vogue Paris*," *Vogue Paris*, February 19, 2020.

23. *Karl: Une histoire de la mode*, op. cit., p. 549.

24. Following the show, Lagerfeld told the press, "I don't even understand the debate [in France]. Since 1904, the church and state have been separate." Despite this stance, however, he expressed reservations about LGBTQIA+ communities becoming bourgeois and distanced himself somewhat from this desire to marry and conform. As he said in an interview with *VICE UK*, "In the sixties, they all said we had the right to the difference [*sic*]. And now, suddenly, they want a bourgeois life."

25. See: www.ericcanto.com/karl-lagerfeld-photographe. Interview first published by *Aperture* magazine, winter 1991.

26. Ibid.

27. *Chanel défilés*, op. cit., p. 19.

CREDITS

ACKNOWLEDGMENTS

Thank you to Chanel, and especially Cécile Goddet-Dirles, Laurence Delamare, and Madeleine Meissirel.

Thank you also to Fendi, particularly Elena Possiedi, Nicoletta Vaccarella, Maria Elena Cima, and Florian Chevallereau.

Thank you to Géraldine Sommier and Maud Villers at Chloé.

Thank you to the magazine *Silhouette*, and to its editorial director, Thomas Aïdan.

And thank you to Camille Dejardin and Marius Corbet for their precious help.

For Abrams:
Editor: Juliet Dore
Design Manager: Darilyn Lowe Carnes
Managing Editor: Amy Vinchesi
Production Manager: Larry Pekarek
Translated from the French by Christopher Bradley

For Éditions E/P/A—Hachette Livre:
Direction: Ariane Lainé-Forrest
Editorial Manager: Boris Guilbert
Creative Director: Clotilde Roussin
Graphic Layout: Giulia Bordignon
Copy Preparation: Nathalie Rachline
Proofreading: Florence Collin
Production: Léa Legentil
Photograving: Hyphen-Media

Library of Congress Control Number has been applied for.

ISBN: 978-1-4197-8734-8
eISBN: 979-8-89684-023-7

Printed and bound in China
10 9 8 7 6 5 4 3 2 1

Abrams books are available at special discounts when
purchased in quantity for premiums and promotions as
well as fundraising or educational use. Special editions
can also be created to specification. For details, contact
specialsales@abramsbooks.com or the address below.

Abrams® is a registered trademark of Harry N. Abrams, Inc.

ABRAMS The Art of Books
195 Broadway, New York, NY 10007
abramsbooks.com

ABRAMS is represented in the UK and Europe by Abrams
& Chronicle Books, 1 West Smithfield, London EC1A 9JU
and Média-Participations, 57 rue Gaston Tessier, 75166
Paris, France.

abramsandchronicle.co.uk and media-participations.com
info@abramsandchronicle.co.uk

MIX
Paper | Supporting
responsible forestry
FSC® C005748